ST. LUCIA

Travel Guide

2024-2025

Your Comprehensive Guide to Explore Caribbean Islands Paradise: Discovering the Beauty and The Natural Wonders.

Victoria J Barham

Copyright © Victoria J Barham,2023.

All rights reserved. No part of this publication may be reproduced, distributed, or transmitted in any form or by any means, including photocopying, recording, or other electronic or mechanical methods, without the prior written permission of the publisher.

Table of Contents

My St Lucia experience
Introduction to St. Lucia
    Geographical Overview
    History and Culture
    Travel Tips
Chapter 2: Planning Your Trip
    When to Visit
    Visa and Entry Requirements
    Budgeting and Costs
    Packing Essentials
    Saint Lucian beach packing list
Chapter 3: Getting to St. Lucia
    Transportation Options
    Airport Information
    Cruise Ship Arrivals
Chapter 4: Accommodations
    Hotels and Resorts
    Villas and Guesthouses
Chapter 5: Exploring St. Lucia
    Top Attractions and Outdoor Activities
Chapter 6: St. Lucian Cuisine
    Local Dishes and Flavors
    Popular Restaurants
Chapter 7: Nightlife and Entertainment

- Bars and Clubs
- Live Music and Events
- Cultural Shows

Chapter 8: Shopping and Souvenirs
- Local Crafts and Art
- Markets and Shopping Districts

Chapter 9: Practical Information
- Health and Safety
- Currency and Banking
- Communication

Chapter 10: Tips for a Sustainable Visit
- Responsible Tourism
- Eco-Friendly Practices

Chapter 11: Language and Culture
- Creole Phrases
- St. Lucia Creole Proverbs
- Cultural Etiquette

Conclusion

My St Lucia experience

The island of St. Lucia, known for its stunning natural beauty, vibrant culture, and kind Caribbean hospitality, has always been a dream of mine. When I eventually set out on my trek to this fascinating location, it was a dream come true. My trip to St. Lucia was nothing short of extraordinary, and I will never forget it.

My trip started when my plane touched down at Hewanorra International Airport, which is located on the southernmost point of the island. I was met with the sight of verdant hills that appeared to go on forever as the aircraft descended. There was a tangible thrill upon entering this tropical haven.

I got a taste of the kind welcome that St. Lucia is renowned for when I arrived at the airport. The airport itself was a tribute to the allure of the island; its open-air layout and vividly colored bougainvillea roof gave me the first impression that I had entered a tropical haven.

During this journey, I slept at a quaint little hotel tucked away amid the majestic Piton Mountains, a UNESCO World Heritage site. Upon entering my accommodation, I was greeted with a vast panorama of the Caribbean Sea's pristine seas and the Pitons. It was a very lovely scene.

I woke up early on my first morning in St. Lucia to the sound of the waves crashing into the coast. I started out on a mission to discover this stunning island's natural beauties since I couldn't resist the lure to explore it. The world's only drive-in volcano, Sulphur Springs, was my first destination.

A pungent sulfur odor pervaded the air, and plumes of steam rose from the Earth, creating an unearthly picture at the Sulphur Springs. I got the opportunity to take a guided tour that covered the area's geothermal activities and even had the opportunity to soak in the mineral-rich pools for a mud bath. It was a refreshing and unusual experience.

I next went to the Diamond Botanical Gardens, which is a verdant haven with colorful plants. The Diamond Waterfall, a multicolored waterfall that empties into a pool of vivid waters rich in minerals, was the focal point. I couldn't help but take a cool swim, and it was the most rejuvenating experience ever.

Beyond the waterfalls and geothermal marvels, St. Lucia had breathtaking natural splendor. There are immaculate beaches with sugar-white sand and crystal-clear seas on the island. Anse Chastanet Beach, which is well-known for its snorkeling and colorful marine life, was one of my favorite locations. I looked around the underwater ecosystem for hours, taking in the vibrant corals and unique animals.

Adventure seekers may also engage in a range of outdoor activities on the island. I made the difficult decision to hike Gros Piton, one of the massive volcanic summits. Although the climb was difficult, I was rewarded with expansive vistas of the island's verdant terrain and the turquoise water that stretched as far as the eye could see.

I went to Pigeon Island National Landmark to continue my research of St. Lucia's natural treasures. Originally a pirate hideaway, this historic monument is now a well-preserved park with hiking paths and insights into the island's colonial past. A unique view into the past was offered by the remains of military fortifications.

Beyond only its breathtaking scenery, St. Lucia has a rich culture and history. I was able to fully immerse myself in the lively Creole culture of the island. I went to the busy Castries Market, which was a sensory joy with its vibrant ambiance, fresh fruit, and handcrafted goods from the area. It was a sensory extravaganza, enhanced by the perfume of spices and the vivid colors of the products on exhibit.

I also got the chance to see a traditional Creole music and dance show when I was in Castries. The vibrancy of the dancers' vibrant clothes and the beat of the drums both spoke to the island's vast cultural diversity. I couldn't help but get involved in the dance, pick up a few Creole movements, and experience what it's like to be a real member of the group.

I had the good fortune to attend a "Friday Night Jump-Up" at Gros Islet one evening. With street vendors selling food, live music, and amiable residents willing to share their island's culture, the streets were turned into a vibrant celebration. I enjoyed the cuisine, which included green fig and saltfish, and I had a great time dancing the night away with my new pals.

Not only was my trip to St. Lucia a time of discovery and cultural immersion, but it was also a period of pampering and relaxation. At one of the opulent resorts on the island, I treated myself to a spa day and had a massage while taking in views of the Caribbean Sea. It was the ultimate in peace and relaxation, the ideal way to decompress.

As my stay in St. Lucia came to an end, I couldn't help but think back on all of the incredible experiences I had had. My heart had been permanently altered by the island. Every moment had been a treasure, from the colorful culture to the natural grandeur of the Pitons and the geothermal springs.

My experience in St. Lucia served as a reminder of the mind-blowing and soul-enriching benefits of travel. I will always cherish the memories I made on the island because of its natural beauty and kind locals. I vowed to return to this magical island at some point in the future to make new memories and rediscover the wonder of my once-in-a-lifetime experience in paradise as I departed St. Lucia full of gratitude.

Introduction to St. Lucia

Geographical Overview

One of the small islands in the Windward Islands archipelago is St. Lucia. Whereas the Bahamas, the Yucatan Peninsula, Florida, and other large limestone areas are composed of small coral-and-sand islands, St. Lucia is a typical Windward Island composition of volcanic rock that formed much later in the region.

St. Lucia's physical features are stunningly beautiful. Steep peaks and deep rain forests dominate the 616 square kilometer island. It is well recognized for the twin peaks of Gros Piton and Petit Piton on the southwest coast, as well as for its beautiful natural harbors and soft sand beaches. With a height of 958 meters above sea level, Mount Gimie is the highest peak in the middle mountain range. The stark variation in climate between coastal and inland areas reflects this distinction. The steep topography draws even more attention to the many rivers that flow from central St. Lucia to the Caribbean. Numerous productive land holdings on the island support the cultivation of bananas.

Because of its tropical, humid climate, which is moderated by trade winds from the northeast, St. Lucia has pleasant year-round weather. The average annual temperature at sea level is between 26 and 32 degrees Celsius, although it may be as low as 13 degrees Celsius at the top of mountains. The abundant annual precipitation amounts to around 200 millimeters, most of which falls during the rainy season, which runs from June to December. A hurricane is the most powerful meteorological phenomenon in this area and has the capacity to cause substantial harm. Although St. Lucia has mostly escaped significant hurricane damage, Hurricane Allen killed nine people and severely damaged the island's agriculture in 1980.

History and Culture

The little island country of St. Lucia has a rich past. Around 350 years ago, Europeans made the first settlement there, and now, a diverse mix of European and African ancestry make up the culture. Although the island's primary industry now is tourism, colonizing European powers were interested in this Caribbean island in order to grow and export crops during the spice trade.

History

The Arawak people, who are said to have arrived by boat from the continent of South America between 200 and 400 AD, were the first inhabitants of the island of St. Lucia. Pottery from archeological investigations has shown evidence of their presence here. Between 800 and 1000 AD, the Carib people—who controlled the majority of the Caribbean islands and are the source of the region's name—started to supplant the Arawaks and stayed until European discovery.

Due to misunderstanding in the paperwork at the time, the precise date of the first European landings on the islands is unknown, although it is believed to have occurred around 1492 or 1502 during the early Spanish empire's excursions. Due to their focus on the wealth of South America, the Spanish had little interest in colonizing the island, and the British had failed in their first efforts at colonization in the 17th century. After signing a pact with the indigenous Carib tribes, the French colonized the islands in 1660 and started growing sugar cane on plantations.

One of the first nations in the Caribbean to be colonized by Europeans was St. Lucia, and as the export of spices and sugar increased, so did the influx of African slaves. The population of African origin far outweighed that of European descent by the time slavery was outlawed in 1834. Ninety-five percent of people in the nation today are of African or mixed African and European ancestry. The percentage of people who identify as Indo-Caribbean is 3%.

Before the British, who by then had an empire that ruled the area, eventually took possession of St. Lucia in 1814, several conflicts had been fought between European troops for sovereignty of the island. It joined the British Windward Islands colony, which lasted until 1958 when it was abolished. Prior to achieving complete sovereignty in 1979, the nation entered a number of alliances but was never really independent.

St. Lucia, which has around 175,000 residents, is still a member of the British Commonwealth and has stable political conditions and a respectable level of life. Although there has been a significant reduction in recent years due to the financial crisis in the US and Europe, tourism remains the island's primary economic activity. Although the export of bananas is a significant contributor to the country's economy, several St. Lucian communities have lately suffered due to growing competition from producers in Latin America.

culture

St. Lucia's culture combines elements of English, French, and African ancestry. For instance, the primary language spoken is English, but due to centuries of French rule, you may also hear people speaking a French patois dialect. The majority of people living in St. Lucia are descended from African slaves, and they follow Roman Catholicism to a considerable extent, but quite generously. Information on the lengthy history of the island is available in the museum at Pigeon Island National Park.

The people of St. Lucian's are very proud of their 1992 Nobel Prize winner, Derek Walcott. In Castries, they named a space in his honor, where the Cathedral of Immaculate Conception is shaded by a 400-year-old samaan tree. Introduced by the British, cricket is the national sport of the country. Darren Sammy, a St Lucian, is now the captain of the regional West Indies cricket team.

Travel Tips

There will be many of chances for visitors to Saint Lucia to engage in a variety of life-changing experiences while being awed by the island's breathtaking scenery. The island's charming surroundings provide the ideal backdrop for a romantic getaway with a special someone. Of all, planning beforehand is the key to a wonderful vacation, regardless of how you decide to spend your time in Saint Lucia.

THE TOP TEN TRAVEL ADVICE FOR SAINT LUCIA

1. Create a vacation Itinerary: The first step in preparing for a vacation is to create a schedule of the things you want to see and do. Making a plan can help you accomplish more of your goals and simplify the process of packing for your vacation. A plan is usually a good idea, but every journey can be made a bit more fun by being adaptable and receptive to new experiences.

2. Make Copies of Vital paperwork: Your ideal trip might soon become a nightmare if you misplace vital paperwork. In case of unanticipated problems, you should prepare clear photocopies of documents such as IDs, passports, and invoices for prepaid services. You may save an enormous lot of time, money, and frustration by following one easy tip.

3. Notify Financial organizations of Your Travel Itineraries - When you travel, you must notify your bank, credit card providers, and other financial organizations. By doing this, you'll avoid having your accounts placed on pause. If you don't, you can run into a lot of problems. You may notify most banks of your intentions using the easy-to-use features in their app.

4. Compare Rates and Prices: If you're planning a trip or staying somewhere, it's definitely worth taking the time to compare prices and rates. Depending on what you're searching for, package offers might save you a lot of money. Remember that certain bonuses, services, and conveniences could be worth the little increase in cost. To get a comparison of costs, choose the "book now" option below and enter the dates you want to visit.

5. Think About Going Off-Season — If you have flexible travel dates, visiting Saint Lucia off-season might result in significant cost savings. There are a ton of amazing events, festivals, and activities happening despite it being the off-season. Actually, this is the busiest time of year on the island and the most probable time to get a genuinely authentic Saint Lucia experience!

6. Create a Packing List: Prior to starting to pack, jot out a list of the items you will need and want for your vacation. Give it some thought as to what you may contribute to improve the activities you have planned. To avoid any surprises when you reach to the airport, find out your airline's baggage rules, weigh your luggage, and confirm their size before you leave.

7. Pack Wisely: Try to bring as much as you think you'll need, but also be realistic and don't fill up important space with stuff you can get anyplace. Instead of folding your garments, roll them firmly to save valuable space and lessen the appearance of deep wrinkles.

Any necessary goods, including as your ID, passport, banknotes, traveler's checks, credit cards, contact details, and prescription drugs, should be carried about at all times or stored in the hotel safe. Additionally, make space in your luggage for mementos!

8. Acquire Knowledge of Some Important Phrases: Although most Saint Lucians, particularly those under 40, speak English well, it's always a good idea to be somewhat bilingual. Although Kwéyòl is mostly spoken in tiny towns and rural areas, there are few expressions that are used all throughout the

island. Although knowing how to communicate well is definitely helpful, having some conversational skills in the language can also make your vacation a bit more enjoyable.

9. Turn on foreign Data on Your Phone: These days, most carriers provide reasonably priced foreign travel packages. For using your data while you're away from home, several of them may charge as little as $10 US each day. However, local carriers Digicel and FLOW both provide affordable travel plans if your current carrier doesn't offer something similar.

10. Save Your Hotel Information: It's also a good idea to save the location, phone number, and room number of your hotel on your phone. Even the most significant information might be easily forgotten with everything going on. This one step may greatly reduce the difficulty of

attempting to find your way around in strange places.

Chapter 2: Planning Your Trip

When to Visit

The ideal time to go to St. Lucia mostly relies on your interests and the experiences you want to have there. However, the dry season, which usually lasts from December to April, is the most well-liked and suggested period to visit St. Lucia. The various seasons and their offerings are broken down as follows:

1. From December to April, the dry season
   - The busiest travel time of year in St. Lucia is now.

- Anticipate good weather with less humidity, perfect for exploration and outdoor activities.
- The ideal weather for taking use of the island's beaches, hiking trails, and water activities is clear sky and mild temps.
- The lively mood is further enhanced by the multitude of cultural festivals and activities that occur during this period.

2. June through November is hurricane season:
- These are the months when St. Lucia enjoys its rainy season, with August and September having the greatest probability of hurricanes or tropical storms.
- Traveling at this time of year is less expensive, but there's a greater chance of rain and schedule interruptions.

- It's crucial to monitor the weather and get travel insurance if you want to visit during these months.

3. November and May are shoulder seasons:
    - The change from the rainy to the dry season occurs throughout these months.
    - Prices could be lower than at the busiest time of year, and pleasant weather with sporadic showers is still possible.
    - For tourists looking for a good mix of affordable prices and comfortable accommodations, now is a terrific time.

In conclusion, the dry season, which runs from December through April, is the greatest time to visit St. Lucia for beautiful weather and a lively environment. But the shoulder seasons of May and November may also be fun if you want less people and can tolerate the possibility of rain. If at all feasible, stay away from the hurricane season since there is a greater chance of unfavorable weather.

Visa and Entry Requirements

Basic guidelines for entering St. Lucia and obtaining a visa. Because immigration laws are subject to change, it is imperative that you confirm the most recent details with the St. Lucian embassy or consulate that is closest to you or visit the official government website for updates:

Visa Requirements:
For brief tourist trips, citizens of several nations are not required to get a visa. The amount of time you are able to enter without a visa, however, varies depending on your country.

You could need a certain kind of visa if you want to work, study, travel, or conduct business while you're in St. Lucia for a prolonged length of time. For information on the suitable visa category, get in touch with the St. Lucian embassy or consulate in your home country.

Passport

All travelers visiting St. Lucia must have a current passport. Make sure your passport is valid for at least six months after the day you want to leave St. Lucia.

Return Ticket:

Immigration officers could request documentation of your return or subsequent travel. Make sure you have a clear itinerary or a copy of your return ticket.

Entry Requirements:

Generally speaking, tourists are only permitted to remain in St. Lucia for a certain amount of time—up to ninety days in most cases. The precise time frame varies based on your country.

Certificate of Yellow Fever (if applicable):
You may need to provide a current yellow fever vaccination certificate upon arrival if you are visiting or are departing from a place where there is a possibility of yellow fever transmission.

Proof of Accommodation:
When you arrive in St. Lucia, it is important to have documentation of your arrangements, such as hotel reservations.

Sufficient Funds:

Immigration officers could question you about how you're going to pay for your stay in St. Lucia. Proof that you have enough money for your vacation could be useful.

It is important to confirm the latest entrance and visa requirements with the official St. Lucia government website or the closest St. Lucian embassy or consulate prior to your travel, since these rules are subject to change. Furthermore, depending on your intended use for the visit (business, tourism, employment, etc.), the criteria for admission may change, so be sure you have the right paperwork for your particular trip.

Budgeting and Costs

The Caribbean country of Saint Lucia is 616 square kilometers in size. With 160,922 residents, it has a density of 261.24 persons per square kilometer. English is the official language, and the GDP of the nation is $1.377 billion. The East Caribbean dollar is used as the unit of money, and the top-level domain is.lc.

Saint Lucia has a rich cultural history and a good standard of living despite its tiny size. Due to the low cost of living, retirees and foreigners find it to be a desirable location. For those who like the great outdoors, the island's moderate temperature, immaculate beaches, and lush tropical landscape are perfect.

Martinique, to the north, and Saint Vincent and the Grenadines, to the south, are the nations that border Saint Lucia. In addition, the island's robust tourist sector makes a substantial economic contribution. All things considered, Saint Lucia is a little yet energetic country that provides a distinctive Caribbean experience.

Estimated Cost of Living in Saint Lucia

Without rent, the total cost of living in Saint Lucia for two individuals with typical consumption for a month would be 1942.93 USD.

Prices at restaurants

Saint Lucia is a cultural melting pot, and this diversity is reflected in its cuisine. Enjoying the island's delicious Creole, Afro-Caribbean, and French-inspired food will be a pleasure for visitors. There is something to suit every appetite, from little, family-run roadside shacks selling delicious jerk chicken to upscale eateries with Michelin-starred chefs. Travelers may enjoy freshly caught seafood meals like grilled lobster and fish cakes, as well as regional specialties like the country's signature dish of green fig and saltfish. Whatever cuisine you're like, Saint Lucia is certain to satisfy your palate.

There are plenty of additional distinctive dining alternatives in Saint Lucia in addition to the usual dining locations. Visitors may reserve a sunset sail and have a three-course dinner while admiring the island's stunning shoreline for a once-in-a-lifetime dining experience. Or, they can decide to have a candlelit, champagne-filled romantic supper on the beach. There are also farm-to-table experiences offered for the more daring eaters, where visitors can taste freshly gathered products right from the source. Whatever your taste may be, Saint Lucia offers plenty of options for both informal dining and opulent culinary excursions.

- Lunch at a Cheap Restaurant $5.15

- Two people's three-course meal at a moderately priced restaurant $ 31.29
- McDonald's McMeal or an other combo meal for $9.20
- Domestic Beer, Draught 0.5 Liter, $1.84
- 3.31 $ for a 0.33-liter bottle of imported beer
- Cappuccino $3.54 $
- Coke (Coca-Cola), 0.33-liter bottle, $0.96

pricing in markets

When compared to other Caribbean islands, Saint Lucia's market pricing is often reasonable. The island's size and location mean that there is a restricted supply of certain items, which might raise their price. But there are many local markets where both tourists and residents may often find more reasonably priced fresh vegetables and handcrafted goods.

Prices for products and services are often higher in the island's tourist hotspots, such as Rodney Bay and Soufriere, than in other locations. This is mostly because more tourists are coming, and they're ready to spend more for the convenience of being in one place. However, travelers to Saint Lucia may discover moderately priced alternatives for lodging, food, and activities with a little study and some exploring off the well-traveled pathways.

- Bottle of water, 0.33 liters, $0.77
- Regular milk, one liter, $2.27
- Fresh White Bread Loaf, 0.5 kg, $0.86
- White rice, 24%, 1 kilogram
- 12 packs of Egg $2.77
- 1 kilogram of local cheese costs $5.46.
- One kilogram of skinless, boneless chicken breasts costs $9.71.

- Round of Beef or Similar Back Leg Red Meat, 1 kilogram, $11.41
- Apples: 1 kilogram at $6.88
- 1 kilogram banana, $1.38
- 1 kilogram oranges for $2.39
- 1 kg of tomato, $4.05
- 1 kilogram potato for $1.99
- 1 kilogram onion, 1.47 $
- One head of lettuce, 1.84 $
- $1.19 for a 1.5-liter bottle of water
- Wine Bottle, Mid-Range Cost: $9.20
- Bottle of domestic beer, 0.5 liters, $1.84
- 3.19 for a 0.33-liter bottle of imported beer
- A pack of smokes $2.58

Costs of transportation

The tiny island country of Saint Lucia has little access to public transit. On the other hand, there are several ways for guests to go about the island. Major cities have plenty of taxis that may be rented for a few hours or a day. Car rentals are another option available to visitors, and they're a great way to see the island at your own speed. A current driver's license and a deposit are needed to rent an automobile. Buses and minivans are examples of public transit that may get you to more rural parts of the island, although they don't always follow a set schedule. Taking a guided tour of the island is one of the most well-liked methods of getting about. A guided tour is a great opportunity to see some of the most stunning and well-known sights on the island while learning about the history, culture, and people of Saint Lucia.

While seeing the stunning coastline of Saint Lucia, visitors might also think about taking a boat transportation option. The greatest ways to see the island's immaculate beaches and blue seas are from a water taxi or a catamaran. While catamarans provide sunset sails and snorkeling excursions, water taxis may transport tourists to remote beaches, fishing towns, and snorkeling locations. A romantic private yacht tour around the island may also be arranged by visitors. It's a great opportunity to de-stress and enjoy the island's stunning surroundings, which includes some of the most gorgeous views in the Caribbean.

- One-way Ticket: $0.93 for Local Transport
- Monthly Pass, Standard Cost $55.23
- Taxi Start, Regular Rate $7.36
- Taxi fare, normal tariff, one-kilometer rate, $22.09
- Taxi, normal tariff, twenty-one dollars for an hour of waiting
- One-liter fuel costs $1.22.

- VW Golf 1.4 90 KW Trendline (Or Similar New Vehicle) $21,170.60

Monthly Rates for Utilities

It's crucial to keep in mind that Saint Lucia may have more expensive utility bills than other places. This is because the island's ability to produce electricity and clean drinking water is mostly dependent on imported fuel. Because of this, guests who stay at resorts or use amenities like air conditioning and hot water showers may see an increase in their energy expenditures. It is thus advised that while planning their budget for their vacation to Saint Lucia, tourists account for these extra expenses.

Saint Lucia's gorgeous beaches, verdant rainforests, and lively culture continue to draw tourists despite the island's increasing utility prices. A lot of resorts and hotels have also made investments in renewable energy sources and adopted water-saving strategies in an effort to become more environmentally friendly. While taking advantage of all Saint Lucia has to offer, travelers may lessen the environmental effect of their trip by making a deliberate effort to limit waste and utilize resources properly.

Basic utilities for an 85 square meter apartment include garbage, water, electricity, and heating or cooling
$ 119.66

Local Prepaid Mobile Tariff, cost per minute, no discounts or plans

Internet, Cable/ADSL, 60 Mbps or faster, Unlimited Data, 46.94 $

Prices for Sports and Leisure

You won't be let down if you're seeking for action and adventure when visiting Saint Lucia. There are many different outdoor sports and activities available on the island to satisfy every kind of visitor. There are plenty of exhilarating activities in Saint Lucia, ranging from zip-lining and trekking through the jungle to world-class diving and snorkeling. For those looking for an even more active holiday, horseback riding, mountain biking, and kayaking are other popular choices. On any of Saint Lucia's many beaches, you may unwind and enjoy the sun if you're looking for a slower-paced experience. There are plenty of sports and recreational activities on the island to keep you occupied throughout your visit, regardless of your hobbies and degree of fitness.

Sports aficionados will find Saint Lucia to be the perfect location due to its distinct geography and natural beauty. The island provides a broad range of water activities, with the Atlantic Ocean to the east and the Caribbean Sea to the west. In the pristine seas, guests may enjoy sailing, windsurfing, kitesurfing, and fishing on charters. There are several well-known diving sites in Saint Lucia where you may see beautiful coral reefs and a variety of marine life. The island is renowned for its nature walks and hiking routes, which allow visitors to explore the rainforests and enjoy breath-taking vistas of the Pitons. Because of Saint Lucia's dedication to sustainable tourism and environmental preservation, you may take part in exciting sports and leisure activities that also respect the environment.

Fitness Club: $35.60 Per Month for One Adult

Pay and Costs of Financing

Depending on the sector and kind of work, Saint Lucia offers several financing and salary options. Since tourism is a significant sector in the nation, many residents work in restaurants, hotels, and resorts. These industries often pay less than other fields, however tips may have a significant impact on income. However, specialists in the IT, healthcare, and finance sectors often make more money. Living costs on the island may be somewhat expensive, and imported items often have higher prices than they would in other nations. Nonetheless, by using neighborhood markets and events, the cost of living might be reduced.

A financial obstacle may also face some tourists or foreigners living in Saint Lucia. Even though the island is home to many large banks, getting credit may be challenging, particularly for those without a history of credit in the area. Furthermore, there's a chance that some services—like online payment methods—are less common in Saint Lucia than they are in other nations. ATMs and currency exchange bureaus are only two of the many places you may get cash and convert currencies. Before visiting any new nation, including Saint Lucia, it's a good idea to investigate your financial possibilities.

One seat cinema ticket, $9.03

Monthly Average Net Salary After Tax: $1,325.47

The mortgage interest rate for a 20-year fixed-rate, annual fixed-rate loan is 1.03 percent.

The cost of childcare

The cost of childcare in Saint Lucia varies based on the provider's location and style. The cost of informal home-based caregivers is often lower than that of schools and kindergartens. On the other hand, the growth of a kid is aided by the highly regimented and instructional programs that these institutions provide. Selecting a daycare provider should take into account both the demands of the kid and the parents' finances.

In Saint Lucia, schools usually provide a full-day curriculum that covers instruction, extracurricular activities, and meals in addition to child care. These establishments provide top-notch services and are manned by qualified specialists that are licensed, regulated, and monitored. In contrast, kindergartens provide a curriculum that is more specifically designed to get kids ready for formal education. There are public and private options available to parents, each with varying entry criteria and tuition costs.

Monthly Cost of Private Preschool or Kindergarten for One Child: 92.06 $

Prices of Clothes and Shoes

There are many different alternatives available in Saint Lucia for shoes and clothes. There are both local and foreign brands accessible on the island. Street sellers, boutiques, and malls all provide fashionable clothing to visitors. They may also get reasonably priced, well-made shoes that are ideal for island exploration. Discounts and promotions are often offered by retailers, particularly during the Christmas season.

Local marketplaces are a good place for tourists to find genuine Saint Lucian apparel. They may buy vibrant, one-of-a-kind goods there that highlight the island's culture. Visitors may also take home fashionable, sustainably crafted handbags and shoes. All things considered, shopping in Saint Lucia is a fun activity that lets guests add some island style to their clothing.

A set of jeans from a chain store, such as Zara, H&M, George, etc.
$ 56.14

Summer Clothing in Chain Stores: Zara, George, H&M, etc.
36.81 USD

Mid-range running shoe pair, priced at 87.44 dollars

A Set of Leather Work Shoes for $111.37

Monthly Rental Prices

Saint Lucia, with its gorgeous beaches, blue oceans, and verdant surroundings, is a paradise just waiting to be discovered. There are many of short-term rental alternatives available to meet your requirements, whether you're seeking for a quick trip or a longer stay. A variety of villas, flats, and cottages are available, all of which provide all the conveniences of home and stunning views of the island's natural splendor.

Saint Lucia's short-term rentals are very affordable, and many of the houses are situated in desirable areas near to the island's main attractions. You're likely to discover something that fits your requirements and budget, whether you're searching for a private villa in the highlands or a beachfront property. The location, size, and facilities of the property all affect the pricing, but you may discover a variety of solutions to suit any budget. So why not reserve your Saint Lucia short-term rental now and begin discovering all that this beautiful island has to offer!

- City center apartment with one bedroom $ 470.39
- One bedroom apartment outside the city $ 320.68
- City center apartment with three bedrooms $ 1,060.79
- Three bedroom apartment outside of city $ 520.46

Packing Essentials

Vacation packing may be a hassle. To unwind and enjoy your time away from home, however, you want to make sure you have everything you need.

I've put up a comprehensive packing list for Saint Lucia to help you enjoy the packing process less stressfully on your next vacation. Everything from clothing to beach items to gadgets is on this list, which will help you have the best possible trip.

So be sure you bring everything on this list, whether you're going to St Lucia for an exciting adventure or a laid-back beach vacation!

Crucial Records for Saint Lucia

The passport
It is crucial to carry your passport to St. Lucia since it serves as identification documentation and is necessary for admittance. You won't be

allowed to enter the nation without it. Your passport must also be valid and no more than six months from expiration. No visa is required for entry into the island for US citizens. If you are traveling abroad, find out from your local embassy what the criteria are for obtaining a visa.

Top Tip: To be safe, take images of all your key papers, save them on your phone, and send them via email to yourself and a backup contact.

Airline Ticket

This one should go without saying: in addition to needing your ticket to board the aircraft, you will also need to present it to immigration officials at St. Lucia upon resuming your journey, thus it is advisable to print it off. It's possible that you lack internet connectivity to view your email or app.

Travel insurance

For everyone who is organizing a vacation overseas, travel insurance is a crucial factor. It may aid with safeguarding against unforeseen medical and financial costs, trip cancellations, and other incidentals that may occur while traveling to Saint Lucia. Loss of luggage, delays, and other unforeseen costs are also covered by some insurances.

Reservations for Hotels

When visiting Saint Lucia, it's crucial to pack your hotel bookings since customs officers can need documentation proving your accommodations. It would be easier for you to submit the required information and prevent any delays in your admission procedure if you have your hotel reservation with you, either printed out or stored as a snapshot on your phone.

Having it printed out is also extremely useful for giving the address to taxi drivers while you're traveling to your hotel.

License to Drive

Having your driver's license with you while visiting Saint Lucia is crucial for many reasons.

Identification: A valid driver's license is one of the most popular kinds of identification that many banks need when doing transactions.

Driving: You must have a current driver's license if you want to hire a vehicle in St. Lucia.

Saint Lucian beach packing list

Swimwear

You should absolutely take your swimming suit for your vacation to Saint Lucia, since you will be spending a lot of time in the water and on the beach. To avoid having to wear a damp swimsuit, remember to pack extra.

Seaside Towel

Beach towels are provided by a lot of hotels and all-inclusive resorts, but you may want to carry your own while traveling to Saint Lucia. Beach towels that dry rapidly and are lightweight make them particularly convenient to store and travel.

Beach towels are also useful for creating a barrier between your skin and the sand and a place to sit or lie down. Another excellent strategy to shield your skin from the sun's rays and keep yourself comfortable in between ocean swims is to carry a beach towel.

Sunglasses

It is essential to have sunglasses while visiting Saint Lucia due to the intense sun. Invest in sunglasses with high UV protection; they will lessen eye fatigue and save your eyes from long-term harm.

I normally pack a more affordable pair for outdoor activities and a nice pair for the beach and strolling around. I can simply replace the inexpensive pair if I break it or misplace it.

Sunglscreen

In addition to wearing sunglasses, you should shield your skin from the intense Caribbean sun. It's essential to pack a strong sunscreen while visiting Saint Lucia's beaches. Seek for an

SPF-rated sunscreen that provides protection from UVA and UVB rays—ideally, triple protection.

Reapply sunscreen every 20 to 30 minutes, more often if you plan to spend a lot of time in the sun. Even if you spend the whole day beneath an umbrella, you might still become sunburned if you don't use sunscreen. I know; I discovered this the hard way.

Shoe Water

For the optimum comfort and safety while swimming in Saint Lucia's ocean, water shoes with a tight fit and strong traction are recommended. Walking barefoot on several of the beaches is painful due to their rough surface. Sea urchins may be seen in the ocean, along with big, jagged pebbles.

Caps

Packing a couple hats is advised since Saint Lucia has year-round heat and sunshine, similar to other Caribbean islands. Sports hats shield your face and head from the sun and are small. An even better choice for sun protection and style points is a hat with a broad brim.

Underwear Cover-Up

Bringing a cover-up for your swimsuit is a smart idea so you won't have to change out of your clothing every time you leave the beach. Because it is required to be worn in public spaces and provides a seamless transition from a beach to a dining or social event, beach packing is especially significant in Saint Lucia. Another effective way to shield your skin from the sun is to wear a cover-up.

Flip-Flops

Beaches and flip-flops go hand in hand, so don't forget to bring some. They are quite lightweight and pack down little, so you won't have to pay extra for them when you check out. Another great choice for when you're out and about touring the resort are flip-flops. You don't have to be concerned about breaking pricey shoes since they are both fashionable and reasonably priced.

Underwater Camera & Accessories

Beautiful reefs, vibrant fish, and crystal pure water may all be found at Saint Lucia. The best option for recording your scuba diving or snorkeling excursions is an underwater camera. I utilize the excellent action camera alternatives from GoPro and DJI Osmo. To make sure you have enough storage, remember to bring extra memory cards and batteries.

Snorkel Equipment

It's recommended to carry your own equipment if you want to snorkel on Saint Lucia's beaches. Fins, a swim cap, goggles, and a snorkel tube make up a whole set. Although most resorts do provide snorkeling equipment for hire, it's always better to bring your own as most of them are old and of poor quality.

Saint Lucian Shoes and Clothes

Easy Outfits

When strolling about the resort, seeing the town, or going on a vacation during the day, casual attire is appropriate. Beachwear, T-shirts, shorts (like khaki or denim shorts), tank tops, short-sleeved shirts, and light pants are some of my suggestions for casual attire in Saint Lucia.

Remember your skirts and sundresses, ladies? For warmer weather, lightweight, breathable materials like cotton or linen work well.

Dress Clothes

Bring some dressier clothing as well, since you will be attending meals, pubs, and clubs. It will look amazing with a long pantsuit and shirt. Don't forget to include several belts and purses as additional accessories.

Sneakers

In addition to flip-flops, you should pack sandals, dressier shoes for evenings out, and durable sneakers or hiking shoes for trips into the surrounding natural areas, such the Rainforest Walk, while visiting Saint Lucia.

Underwear and Pajamas

Of course, we also need to remember the essential underwater and a place to sleep. It's usually a good idea to pack extra underwear in hotter areas.

Rain Jacket

It does rain sometimes in Saint Lucia, particularly during the rainy season, so bring a lightweight jacket in case of sudden downpours. On chilly mornings, you may even use it as a windbreaker.

Cash and Transfers to Saint Lucia

Money

Legal money in Saint Lucia is the Eastern Caribbean Dollar, however U.S. Major credit cards, dollars, and traveler's checks are also accepted. I wouldn't use the ATMs at the airport, but I would still carry cash or withdraw some from one.

For safety reasons, don't carry about your holiday money wherever you go; instead, keep the majority of it in the hotel safe. Pickpockets are a common sight in tourist areas, and their goal is to steal your belongings. Cash is required for tipping, local markets, transportation, and shopping for mementos.

Credit cards

In Saint Lucia, many hotels, resorts, and large eateries accept credit cards. However, to be sure they do not prevent transactions in Saint Lucia, you may wish to verify with your credit card provider and put in a vacation notice. Using a credit card that doesn't charge international transaction fees is also a smart choice, particularly if it offers travel benefits.

Top Tip: When making a payment, always choose the local currency rather than the US dollar if requested to do so. In this manner, you save a tonne of money since your local bank converts currencies at the daily rate.

Journey Wallet

A travel wallet is a handy and safe method to keep your belongings organized while you're on the go. I utilized a variety of them, including neck wallets, bigger carriers that could accommodate passports, and tiny pouches that could contain cash and credit cards.

It keeps everything you need readily accessible and organized. Having a travel wallet might assist you from losing your belongings outright or being pickpocketed in busy places.

Electronics and Chargers for Saint Lucia

An electrical device charger

Because you will be using your electronic gadgets a lot throughout your vacation in Saint Lucia, it is imperative that you pack chargers for them. They will be necessary for you to browse and snap photos and movies. A 12V car charger is also required if you want to hire a vehicle.

Additionally, remember to bring along all necessary cords and your GoPro charger.

Protective Phone Case

A water-resistant or waterproof cover made specifically to shield your mobile device from harm is called a phone protective case. The majority of phones make the claim that they are dust- and water-resistant, but you should cover your phone since salt water is very corrosive and getting sand in your charging port may completely destroy it.

Because Saint Lucia has a humid environment and you will be spending a lot of time on the beach, these cases are quite helpful while visiting there. Additionally, they have neck straps to prevent phone loss while participating in island activities.

E-reader

If you like reading, bring an e-reader with offline book downloads. Because of its unique screen, the e-Reader can be used in direct sunlight, unlike phones or tablets, and its battery lasts considerably longer. It also won't overheat.

Although it still can't match the tactile experience of a real book, it's the greatest option for travel because of luggage restrictions and airlines' increased enforcement of overweight costs.

Power Adapter

Regretfully, each lodging in Saint Lucia has a different electrical outlet. While some people utilize the 110V US plug, the British (220V) outlet is the most often used. It is advisable to have one or more universal adapters with you in order to guarantee that all gadgets may be charged.

Battery Power bank

When there are no other power sources around, you may charge your gadgets while you're on the road with the help of a power bank, which is a portable battery that stores energy. This is quite helpful while traveling, especially whether you're on an airline, at an airport, or just enjoying the area.

Your phone will capture hundreds of pictures, so you'll need to recharge it more often than usual. Invest in a tiny power bank; they are lightweight and portable, making them convenient to carry along.

Saint Lucian toiletries and medications

Personal hygiene

It's crucial to make sure you are ready and have all the toiletries you'll need while visiting Saint Lucia. Hotels often provide shampoo and shower gel, but unless it's a five-star establishment, the quality is generally rather low, so bring your own or get some from the neighborhood store.

You must provide your own toothpaste, toothbrush, perfume, makeup, and other necessary hair care items. Remember to include any supplies you may need for personal hygiene as well.

Essential Medication

In addition to over-the-counter meds like ibuprofen and aspirin, stomach cures, antihistamines, seasickness medication, and any other pills you may require, remember to bring along any prescription drugs you may need. Have your medicines on hand in case the police or TSA want to see them, and keep any prescription drugs in their original bottles.

Body Lotion

It's crucial to take a body lotion that hydrates and leaves your skin feeling moisturized all day while traveling to Saint Lucia in order to shield your skin from the heat. Seek for lotions that include glycerin, shea butter, and hyaluronic acid.

After Sun Cream

Sunscreen, hats, and beach umbrellas won't protect you from the sun entirely. When traveling to tropical regions, I usually pack an Aloe Vera After-Sun Cream since it helps calm and cool the skin.

Insect Repellent

Mosquitoes may be found anywhere. Take some bug repellent cream or spray with you, and avoid letting them spoil your trip, since they are a persistent cause of irritation and itching. There are insect repellents using DEET as an ingredient that work well against mosquitoes, midges, and no-see-ums. There are natural substitutes, but if you happen to be the one in the group who gets stung the most, invest in DEET.

Additional Things to Think About When Packing for St. Lucia

In-Flight Essentials

The duration of the flight might range from one to several hours, depending on your point of departure. In order to make the trip to Saint Lucia more pleasant, I always bring along a few necessities on the plane. My essential items include a face mask, neck cushion, e-reader, earplugs, headphones, hand sanitizer, travel bidet, and my prescription.

Tiny First Aid Package

When I travel, I always have a little first aid kit with me. When I go exploring, I often acquire little scrapes and bruises, particularly in Saint Lucia's tropical jungle. It's a compact, carry-along container that holds necessary supplies including bandages, antiseptic wipes, antibiotic cream, and painkillers.

Travel bag

Wow, travel bags are great. They are lightweight, water-resistant, multi-pocketed, and an essential piece of gear for every traveler, particularly to Saint Lucia. All of your goods, including clothing, toiletries, electronics, and other things you could require for your vacation, can be carried with its assistance.

Taking your items to the beach, sightseeing, or a quick trip is made simpler when you have a lightweight day bag or beach bag. To ensure you get the most out of your trip in Saint Lucia, fill your bag to the brim but don't go crazy.

lockable luggage

All of your belongings will remain safe and secure with the assistance of luggage locks. Thieves and pickpockets search for the most vulnerable victim. Usually, locks on your roller bags and backpacks deter intruders from attempting to access them.

Because locks assist keep your baggage safely closed, they may also prevent your goods from being misplaced or damaged during the trip. There is no excuse not to utilize them since they are inexpensive and tiny to purchase.

Packing Cubes

This is my go-to tactic for maintaining organization. Packing cubes are specialized bags made to make it easier to move, store, and arrange your clothes and other possessions neatly. Typically constructed from sturdy, lightweight fabrics like polyester or nylon, these cubes are portable and stack well in baggage.

They include a lot of useful features that make packing and organizing our items easier, such as labels, mesh windows and pockets, and several sections. To keep your soiled items separate from your clean ones, many sets also include shoe and laundry bags.

Chapter 3: Getting to St. Lucia

Transportation Options

To facilitate your navigation around the island, St. Lucia has a range of transportation choices.

Via Automobile

Visitors must get a temporary driving license for rental automobiles, which they may do at the airport, the police station in Castries, or the car rental companies with a valid driving license. Rental vehicle agencies, hotels, and airports are the places to make reservations for rental cars and scooters. The average daily rate is $50.

In St. Lucia, drivers must travel on the left side of the road. The roads here have several hairpin curves; proceed with caution and beep your horn as you round the bends.

Via minibusses

For locals, the primary mode of ground transportation across much of the island is provided by privately operated minibusses. Along the journey, the routes make stops in between the major towns, forming a large circle around the island. Although bus schedules vary by route, most buses operate until around 7 p.m. (with the exception of the heavily trafficked Castries-Gros Islet line, where they operate until beyond 10 p.m.). On Sundays, buses are not in service. The fare range is $1–$3. Green number plates with a M prefix are used on minibuses.

Buses are only allowed to halt at authorized bus stops in metropolitan areas. If there isn't a bus stop close by in a rural location, you may flag busses down wherever they are traveling as long as there is room for them to stop. Call out 'stopping driver' far in advance of your stop to indicate that you wish to get off.

Via Taxi

St. Lucian taxis are identified by a blue license plate with the prefix "TX." Verify the fare before hiring a cab. Cross-island fares in taxis may run you anything from $80 to $90. From the airport to Marigot Bay, fares are around $70. The number of passengers, the company, the destination, and the quantity of baggage all affect the rate. Be aware that pricing might be considerably negotiated for longer trips. Saint Lucia Taxi Service, Saint Lucia Executive, Saint Lucia Airport Shuttle, Real Saint Lucia Tours, and many more are some of the main taxi services available on the island.

Via Cycling

It's not the easiest area to ride a bicycle in St Lucia. Many roads are small, have little lighting, and have no wide shoulders. Moreover, drivers often fail to provide adequate distance for bicycles since they are not used to seeing them on the road.

Via Boat

On the west side of the island, one may rent a water taxi to go almost anyplace. The most well-traveled routes are from Rodney Bay in the north to Marigot Bay or Soufrière in the south.

Airport Information

When you first arrive in St. Lucia, you will quickly realize that it is one of the most stunning islands in the Caribbean. Additionally, St. Lucia has many airports, which is uncommon for an island of that size. Travelers visiting St. Lucia from other parts of the globe arrive and leave from Hewanorra International Airport, while locations within the Caribbean are served by George F. L. Charles Airport.

1. International Airport of Hewanorra

- Location: Hewanorra Airport, also referred to as UVF Airport, is situated near Vieux Fort, 40 miles south of Castries, the country's capital.

- Best if: You are a guest from outside the Caribbean who is traveling abroad.

- Avoid If: If you are coming from anywhere other than the Caribbean and don't have a private aircraft (which is still terrible for the environment), you will have to go via the airport. However, you may arrange a helicopter shuttle to George F. L. Charles Airport, which is situated in Castries, the country's capital, if you would rather not have to wait in traffic to get to your ultimate destination.

- Distance to Soufriere: The Pitons' residence, Soufriere, is an hour's cab trip from UVF airport. Starting fares are $65. It takes around an hour and a half by taxi to go from Hewanorra International Airport to the island's Rodney Bay region.

With only one terminal, Hewanorra International Airport serves as the main entry point for tourists from abroad. The airport serves a range of airlines including American Airlines, British Airways, Delta, Air Canada, United Airlines, and JetBlue and welcomes direct flights from many U.S. locations. Early in 2019, a $175 million reconstruction project got underway, resulting in a substantially bigger terminal.

Once they get on the island, harried tourists don't have to worry about having trouble finding ground transportation. Travelers will be able to find taxis at both airport sites. Additionally, visitors may travel about the island in style by using the minibus system to get to their accommodation. On the other hand, those who would rather arrange their trips well in advance could think about scheduling a shuttle to their lodging via Saint Lucia Airport Transfers or Saint Lucia Airport Shuttle. Whichever way you choose, be sure to check the fee with your taxi driver ahead of time since it might vary depending on the distance to the hotel, the number of people riding with you, and the quantity of baggage you have.

2. The airport at George F. L. Charles

- Location: George F. L. Charles Airport is situated 1.2 miles (2 kilometers) north of Castries, the country's capital, on Peninsular Road.

- Best if: You're visiting different islands in the Caribbean. boarding flights between islands.

- Avoid If: When making travel arrangements, George F.L. Charles Airport is not an option if you are a tourist from somewhere else in the globe since it does not provide flights to locations outside of the Caribbean Sea. That is, however, an option if you want to reserve a helicopter service for when you arrive (or leave) in St. Lucia from Hewanorra International to George F.L. Charles.

- Distance to Soufriere: Soufriere is also around an hour's drive from George F. L. Charles. Nevertheless, for those who want a better view of the island's verdant, mountainous splendor, we still advise booking a helicopter journey.

When it comes to handling flights between islands, George F. L. Charles Airport is a notably smaller operation than Hewanorra International. The airport, which has only one terminal, serves tropical airlines such Air Antilles, LIAT, Caribbean Airlines, Air Sunshine, and Air Caraibes. Flights to neighboring locations such Saint Kitts, Nevis, Anguilla, Dominica, Antigua, Saint Thomas, and Port of Spain are hosted by George F.L. Charles.

The Caribbean Sea is visible from the airport's lush runway. It is a wonderful experience for travelers to land surrounded by such tropical paradise, with the ocean on three sides and the jungles beyond. George F. L. Charles is an ideal destination if you're on a Caribbean safari and want to see a few more island countries before flying back home.

St. Lucia's airports are less crowded than those of its neighbors, and for those in a hurry or for those who just want to see the Pitons from above, it is even possible to arrange a helicopter transport between the two. Those who are interested in jet-setting (or helicopter hedonistic) should get further information from the St. Lucia tourist office beforehand and schedule a late-arriving return flight to George F. L. Charles Airport the day before they leave.

Cruise Ship Arrivals

The arrival of cruise ships has a major role in St. Lucia's tourist economy. Cruise ships often stop at the island, drawing tourists from all over the globe. An outline of cruise ship arrivals at St. Lucia is shown below:

Ports: There are two main cruise ports in St. Lucia:

- Castries Port: One of the busiest cruise ports in the Eastern Caribbean is the Port of Castries. Situated in Castries, the capital city, it offers convenient access to the city's eating, shopping, and cultural activities.

- Port Vieux Fort: Situated in the southern part of the island, close to Vieux Fort, lies the Hewanorra International Airport. It is mostly an airport, although sometimes cruise ships arrive as well.

Cruise Lines: A wide range of cruise lines are welcomed at St. Lucia, including smaller luxury and boutique cruise lines and larger lines like

Royal Caribbean, Carnival, and Norwegian Cruise Line.

Arrival Schedule: Throughout the year, cruise ships arrive at various periods; the peak season usually lasts from November to April. You should anticipate more frequent arrivals throughout this time. A single day, the island may receive many ships.

Shore Excursions: There are many different shore excursions available to cruise guests. These might include trips to see the island's natural landmarks, such the Pitons and Sulphur Springs, cultural events in Castries and Soufrière, excursions involving the water, like zip-lining and trekking, and adventure tours.

Terminal Facilities: Cruise guests may take advantage of duty-free shopping, eating choices, and tourist information centers at both cruise ports. At the ports, taxis and excursions are easily accessible modes of transportation.

Visa Requirements: For brief stays in St. Lucia, cruise guests often do not need a visa as long as they remain within the time frame given by the cruise company.

Safety and Health Measures: Arrivals of cruise ships have adjusted to comply with health and safety regulations, particularly after the COVID-19 epidemic. Before disembarking, passengers could be subject to safety procedures and health tests.

Even for visitors with limited time on the island, cruise ship arrivals provide a fun and easy opportunity to take in St. Lucia's natural beauty and culture. During their short visits, tourists may see everything that St. Lucia has to offer—from its breathtaking natural beauty to its bustling cities and historical monuments.

Chapter 4: Accommodations

Hotels and Resorts

When searching for the ideal beach vacation, sunseekers visiting the Caribbean have an abundance of options, but St. Lucia is a popular choice. Its famous Piton Mountains, two volcanic peaks set in a valley recognized as a Unesco World Heritage Site, contribute to this. In addition, it is the location of the world's first drive-in volcano and the dream come true for anybody who like chocolate, since Hotel Chocolat offers real hotel chocolate here.

Its volcanic beaches, fishing towns, waterfalls, and capital harbor of Castries are all open for exploration by tourists. The island country in the east Caribbean is well-liked by both scuba divers and birdwatchers.

1. Jade Mount

An episode of the BBC series showcases Jade Mountain as one of the most incredible hotels in the world. At the summit of the Anse Chastanet resort, this architectural marvel seems as if it belongs on a another planet because of its Jurassic Park meets Bond villain lair style.

Where else in the world can you find an infinity pool within your bedroom? These are no typical suites. And by full length pool—all of which are open-air—we mean a pool that runs from the bathroom to the villa's missing fourth wall. There are winding pathways leading to the tumbling suites, and the sound effect of vibrant stained-glass windchimes plays throughout.

The Celestial Terrace, located on the restaurant's roof, is the ideal place to enjoy a sundowner. However, the view of the Piton from your own pool is unbeatable. Diners may eat tacos, ceviche, and huge coconut prawns on the restaurant terrace below, all paired with refreshing rosé wine. The Emerald estate, the hotel's organic farm in the Soufriere hills, provides a large portion of the vegetables. In-room eating (as well as everything else) may be arranged by your Major-Domo if you would like to remain in your Sanctuary.

2. Sugar Beach

Sugar Beach is the kind of vacation paradise where you could spend weeks without getting bored. It really has it all. When you arrive by boat, you can go right to the beach's watersports club, which is handy for planning all of the things you want to do while you're there, including snorkeling and tubing. Though you have been seeing them from a distance, Sugar Beach places you in a secluded cove situated between the two Pitons, one of which resembles King Kong when seen from a certain angle.

The estate, which was once held by Lord Glenconner, was formerly a sugar plantation and is currently home to a daily English afternoon tea. The therapies offered at the rainforest spa, which is housed in different treehouses divided by pathways under the canopies, are inspired by the surrounding environment.

With apartments that sleep up to eight people each and a private stairway going down to the beach, the resort is a fantastic choice for large gatherings. Each cottage, bungalow, or villa features an own plunge pool in addition to butler service. You'll need to use the automobiles that can transport you up and down the estate's 100 acres of jungle (the pastel pink one is the obvious pick to try and shotgun).

Plenty of eateries to choose from, which is convenient for longer visits. Despite being on a Caribbean island, The Cane Bar is a stylish sushi and drink spot that would feel right at home in any major metropolis. The Great Room is the ideal location for a romantic supper, while the Jalousie grill on the beach is great for outdoor barbecues with great drinks before and after.

3. Anse Chastanet

Located just below Jade Mountain and extending all the way to the coast, Anse Chastanet was among the island's first upscale resorts. It was first founded in 1968 and has the same genuine, carefree Caribbean vibe, complete with traditional local textiles, rustic décor, and personnel that wants you to be as happy as they are.

Before the cocoa trees were established, the area was a sugarcane plantation; there are still many of them on the grounds, and the estate uses their fruits to make its own chocolate. Mango, cashews, tamarind, turmeric, and other organic produce are still produced on the property.

Up above are early prototypes of its sister property's outstanding open-air suites, with rooms here featuring wall-free views of two bays. The 600-acre resort offers a variety of seaside activities, such as windsurfing, kayaking, paddle boarding, snorkeling, cycling in the jungle, hiking in the Anse Mamin valley (which offers additional opportunities for bird watching), and windsurfing. However, the weekly sunset jazz cruise, which features a saxophonist serenading the guests, is unquestionably the highlight.

4. Body Holiday

One of the top health vacations in the world is called Body Holiday, and its catchphrase is "Give us your body for a week and we'll give you back your mind." Every guest's itinerary is unique, so the results may be anything you like.

There is an ayurveda temple where patients may get holistic and ayurvedic treatments in addition to acupuncture and Bhutanese ceremonies. Pilates, yoga, tai chi, golf, tennis, archery, cycling, windsurfing, water skiing, and kayaking are all options for staying (or becoming) in shape.

5. Hotel Chocolat

If one were to take the brand name literally, this would be the hotel version of the premium chocolate, a haven for chocolate lovers. Overlooking the Pitons, the six-acre Rabot Estate is located in St Lucia. Before learning how to make their own chocolate bars, visitors may participate in Project Chocolat, an agricultural-tourism experience that teaches them about the growth of cacao and gives them a tour of the rainforest groves. There will also be street cuisine and drinks made with cacao, as well as beauty items and alcohol enriched with chocolate.

6. Cap Maison

Cap Maison, located at Rodney Bay's waterfront, has a restaurant that serves both residents and visitors, along with its own private sandy beach. With columns, terracotta tiles, and rooftop pools, the hotel is made up of several homes and outbuildings.

Since the island is a yearly honeymoon hotspot, hotels here have to step it up to wow newlyweds. At Cap Maison, for example, diners may enjoy a romantic meal in a secluded beachfront setting lighted by tiki torches and candlelight, while zipwiring champagne delivery. This lovely location is of course ideal for sunset viewing, with views of Pigeon Island and Martinique in the background.

7. Ladera Resort

Situated atop a volcanic ridgeline, 1,000 feet above the Caribbean Sea, and within a Unesco World Heritage Site, Ladera Resort is one of the island's most distinctive hotels. Every accommodation has an outside private plunge pool for an unobstructed view of the island's famous peaks, and The Pitons are situated right in front of it. Some have an extra touch of originality with a swing hung over the pool.

Additionally, the rooms include an open wall that showcases the dramatic background, allowing guests to fully take advantage of the breathtaking location. The rooms are created from tropical hardwoods and feature furnishings designed by St Lucian craftsmen.

8. East winds

Stay at East Winds, an all-inclusive resort in St Lucia with 30 cottages, a beach house on the coast, a private beach, and a restaurant by the sea where you can eat the fish of the day served with veggies from the kitchen garden or local farmers. The décor is traditional Caribbean, with white-wood vaulted ceilings, ceiling fans, vibrant drapes and pillows, and serene verandas.

Bird watchers love St. Lucia, and a variety of colorful animals visit East Winds. Don't forget your binoculars, twitchers.

Villas and Guesthouses

For visitors looking for lodging alternatives outside of conventional hotels and resorts, St. Lucia has a variety of villas and guesthouses to choose from. These substitutes provide a more personal and often affordable way to see the island. An overview of St. Lucia's villas and guesthouses is provided below:

Villas:

Private Villas: Private villas in St Lucia range in size from comfortable one-bedroom retreats to expansive multi-bedroom estates. These villas often include breathtaking views, private pools, and all the conveniences you need for a relaxing vacation.

Resort Villas: Villas are an option at several of St. Lucia's upscale resorts. In addition to offering access to the resort's amenities and services, these villas often provide a high degree of seclusion and personalized attention.

Villa Communities: There are specific villa communities in several parts of St. Lucia where you may rent a private villa with access to common spaces like restaurants, swimming pools, and even private beaches.

Self-Catering Villa: Many villas have fully functional kitchens, which makes them perfect for guests who would rather prepare their own meals. This can be a more affordable choice for extended visits.

Guesthouses:

Local Guesthouses: Numerous locally owned guesthouses in St. Lucia provide a more genuine and customized experience. Usually, these guesthouses are owned and operated by amiable people who are eager to impart their local expertise.

Boutique Guesthouses: In St. Lucia, there are guesthouses that provide a boutique experience with distinctive furnishings, attentive service, and careful attention to detail. They may have fewer rooms, which would make it seem more personal.

Bed and Breakfasts: On the island, there are quaint bed and breakfast establishments. These provide a homey atmosphere and usually include breakfast in the lodging charge.

Eco-Friendly Accommodatio: Eco-friendly guesthouses in St. Lucia provide an experience focused on nature and sustainable methods.

<u>**Advantages of lodging at St. Lucian villas and guesthouses:**</u>

Personalized Service: A more individualized and attentive degree of service is often provided by villas and guesthouses.

Personal space: Particularly villas provide a great lot of seclusion, which makes them perfect for families, groups of friends, or couples.

Local Experience: A closer connection to the local way of life and culture may be had by staying at a guesthouse.

Cost Reductions: Budget-friendly choices include guesthouses and self-catering villas, particularly for extended visits.

Unique Atmosphere: St. Lucia offers a variety of villas and guesthouses with distinctive architecture, breathtaking views, and a special atmosphere that will make your stay unforgettable.

It's crucial to do your homework and read reviews before making a reservation for a villa or guesthouse in St. Lucia to make sure it meets your requirements and preferences. Furthermore, take into account the accommodation's location to make sure it fits both your intended island activities and travel schedule.

Chapter 5: Exploring St. Lucia

Top Attractions and Outdoor Activities

One of the most stunning locations on the planet is this island in the Caribbean. Saint Lucia is a nature lover's dream come true with its volcanic beaches, waterfalls, and rainforests.

Not only that, but adventurers, foodies, and history fans will find no shortage of activities in Saint Lucia.

To help you get the most out of your vacation, I've included a list of the top 25 activities to do in Saint Lucia in this chapter.

Here are the greatest activities to do in Saint Lucia, ranging from trekking to the summit of Gros Piton to visiting the Soufriere volcano:

1. Go to the Pitons.
The Pitons are two breathtakingly beautiful volcanic peaks located in St. Lucia. Their imposing presence commands the scenery and creates a memorable experience. Everyone should visit them as they are regarded as one of the island's most stunning locations.

In addition to their breathtaking beauty, the Pitons provide a variety of hiking paths that, for the daring, you may explore. Another fantastic option to come up close and take in the Pitons' spectacular splendor from many perspectives is to take a catamaran cruise around them.

2. Experience Kayaking in Rodney Bay

A great way to take in the serene beauty of the Caribbean is to go kayaking at Rodney Bay, Saint Lucia. You will be able to enjoy the serene bay waters as well as the breathtaking views of the Labrelotte Point shoreline, the lively Pigeon Island National Park, and the surrounding hills.

Rodney Bay's placid waters make it an ideal place for novices to practice and pick up kayaking skills. Many seasoned kayakers are also available to help you make the most of your adventure.

There are also retail centers and marinas in Rodney Bay, so you may take use of these amenities before or after your kayaking excursion.

Along with a wide selection of pubs and clubs, there are several restaurants to choose from when planning a great night out. In addition, the well-known Reduit Beach is not far away if you're seeking for further beach activities.

3. Enjoy a Stunning Drive Through the Rural Area

Enjoy the breathtaking scenery of Saint Lucia's countryside while taking a leisurely drive in an SUV or, for the daring, an exhilarating ATV trip. Take an all-terrain vehicle for a journey around the island and explore the north and south's gorgeous routes.

Discover the island's greatest scenery, small communities, and banana plantations. Discover some agricultural remnants, follow the turtles on the beach, and get insight into the way of life in the area. You may be certain that your off-road experience will be the highlight of your vacation if you choose a reputable tour operator.

4. See the Market in Gros-Islet.
Visitors may have a unique experience and fully immerse themselves in the local way of life at the Gros-Islet Market in Saint Lucia. This fishing hamlet comes alive on Friday nights, with Dauphin Street emanating the smell of grilled seafood and barbecue.

It's difficult to resist the enticing mood created by the bustling streets' row of fishing shacks and rum stores, where fishing nets are left to dry in the sun. You may enjoy the mouthwatering regional food, socialize and dance with the people, and get insight into authentic island culture.

You may find great local vegetables and artisanal products at the Gros-Islet Market, along with handcrafted items and souvenirs. Fresh produce, spices, and other goods harvested directly from the island's fields and trees are available for purchase at the market.

Because there are so many emporiums offering handcrafted goods, it's also an excellent spot to pick up souvenirs and mementos. On a Saturday morning, when the market is busiest and most full of sellers and customers, is the ideal time to go shopping.

5. Take an outdoor tram ride to see St. Lucia's forest canopy.

Taking an open-air tram ride to see St. Lucia's forest canopy is an incredibly unique and captivating experience. A guide goes with every group of guests as they ride the about 16 open-air gondolas into the high forest of the ecological park on a tramway hung about 120 feet above the emerald-green jungle.

Along with the island's unique flora, which include colorful heliconia and enormous ferns, you may identify a variety of birds by their sounds, songs, and feathers as you ride through the forest. Flying over the verdant tree canopy is an amazing experience that offers a close-up, personal look at the natural environment. If you're fortunate, you may even be able to glimpse the St. Lucia parrot, the show's star!

The best way to appreciate St. Lucia's natural beauty and abundant animals is to take an aerial tram ride.

6. Explore the Anse La Raye paths.

Anse La Raye's paths are a fantastic experience, with a variety of lush rainforests and breathtaking vistas. All skill levels of hikers will love the paths, which provide fantastic opportunities to discover the island's many ecosystems. Hikers can immerse themselves in nature and enjoy the breathtaking views from the Roseau Dam Trail, which features winding paths and colorful parrots, to the Des Cartiers Trail and the Tet Paul Nature Trail.

For those looking for a more adventurous outdoor experience, Anse La Raye's paths are excellent. The 45-minute moderate climb on the Roseau Dam Trail gives breathtaking views at the summit and an opportunity to see some of the local fauna.

The Des Cartiers Trail's meandering trails and thick jungle make it an excellent choice for those seeking a more daring adventure. Last but not least, the Tet Paul Nature Trail offers a serene experience and has a well designated trail that leads to breathtaking views of the nearby islands.

There are also a number of waterfalls in this area, including River Rock Waterfalls and Anse La Raye Falls. Even though these are not the most spectacular waterfalls I have seen, the whole family will love visiting and exercising at these magnificent places.

In addition to offering physical exercise, the paths of Anse La Raye provide visitors a chance to learn about the local way of life. In the fishing town, you may socialize with the residents and take part in the Friday Night Fish Fry festivities.

7. Take a Zip-Lining Tour Through the Treetops

In Saint Lucia, zip line through the treetops is a thrilling adventure that provides amazing views of the verdant jungle.

We did the Adrena-Line Canopy Tour at the Treetop Adventure Park, which consists of 12 zip lines that are the tallest and longest on the island. You can see the diverse creatures below as you fly over the canopy, and you can also enjoy the vivid hues of the surrounding plants. In addition, you may trek four paths, cross 20 obstacle platforms, and explore the tropical jungle.

The Morne Coubaril Historical Adventure Park, with its zipline canopy experiences, is also a fantastic alternative. In addition to five net bridges, the Treetop Canopy Adventure has some of the quickest zip lines on the island.

Try the aerial gondola ride to enjoy the scenery without any of the thrills while taking in the coziness of the rainforest.

8. Take a Snorkel or Dive with the Reef Fish

With its enormous coral reefs encompassing almost half of the island's coastline and an abundance of dive spots to explore, diving and snorkeling in Saint Lucia provide an incredibly unique and fascinating experience.

All people may easily participate in snorkeling, and some of the greatest locations include Marigot Bay, the foot of the Pitons, and the Anse Chastanet reef. Numerous marine creatures, including sergeant majors, trumpet fish, angelfish, sea turtles, and hundreds of other kinds of vibrant fish, are available for you to get up close and personal with here.

Popular diving locations for experienced divers include the Soufriere Marine Reserve, the coastal reefs of Pigeon Island National Park, Turtle Reef, Pinnacles, Anse Chastanet Reef, Fairy Land, and Piton Wall. Amongst the coral pinnacles and volcanic rocks, you may see moray eels, eagle rays, lobsters, and many more species.

In addition to providing free dives and top-notch equipment for visitors, several all-inclusive resorts in Saint Lucia also assign qualified dive guides to accompany you on the dive and teach you the fundamentals.

9. Visit Splash Island Water Park with your kids.

Situated on the stunning Reduit Beach in Rodney Bay, Splash Island Water Park provides a plethora of recreational opportunities and kid-friendly amenities. While you relax on lounge chairs beachfront, your kids may have fun in the lifeguard-supervised floating obstacle course.

For younger ones to explore, there are plenty of trampolines, climbing walls, swings, slides, monkey bars, double rockers, hurdles, and a water volleyball court.

10. Play around the golf.

A visit to the Sandals Golf & Country Club in Cap Estate is highly recommended if you're seeking for an enjoyable and challenging golf day. This championship golf course is a terrific location for a game of golf, including a 6,829-yard, par-71 layout and plenty of surrounding vegetation. A day on the greens may be made even more enjoyable by taking advantage of the preferential tee times and free transportation provided by a number of the neighboring resorts.

11. Take a Catamaran Sightseeing Tour to See the Coast.

An incredible experience may be had on a catamaran sightseeing trip of Saint Lucia's coastline. We went on an eight-hour trip that lasted the whole day and included a buffet lunch, rum cocktails, and a variety of activities including ziplining, seeing a cocoa plantation, driving up a volcano, and snorkeling in many locations.

On your way back, you pause to go snorkeling as you cruise around Marigot Bay and take in the aerial views of the Pitons. The cherry on top is a leisurely, romantic sunset voyage back to port, complete with champagne and the opportunity to watch the elusive "green flash" as the sun sets.

12. Hike the Trails of Morne Fortune

Numerous old military strongholds, monuments, and structures may be seen atop Morne Fortune, a famous hill near Castries, St. Lucia. One of the most popular and well-known hiking paths in all of St. Lucia is located on the hill: the Tet Paul Nature Trail. Along with providing an opportunity to see the old defenses and structures, the walk gives breathtaking views over Martinique, the bay, and Castries.

The Tet Paul Nature Trail is well-liked for its diverse topography and constantly changing landscape. The route is a wonderful opportunity to see the beauty of the nation as it leads walkers through a varied terrain of lush, tropical flora with breathtaking views of the Caribbean Sea. The Morne Blanc cascade, a breathtaking natural cascade that is a favorite of both hikers and visitors, is also located along the walk.

A rare chance to learn about and experience the rich history and culture of St. Lucia is provided by the hiking trails of Morne Fortune. Well worth the trek are the stunning vistas and variety of flora and animals. The trails are also a fantastic opportunity to explore the area, keep active, and reconnect with nature.

13. Explore the Botanical Gardens

Tropical flora and gardens may be seen at the lovely Botanical Gardens in St. Lucia. One of the island's oldest and best-preserved homes, the Soufriere Estate, includes the gardens. You may learn about the natural flora and medicinal plants by going on a guided tour of the gardens.

Part of Sulphur Springs Park, the Diamond Falls Botanical Gardens are situated in a protected canyon at the base of the Pitons. The area's rich volcanic soil provides nourishment for an amazing array of tropical flowers and plants.

Visitors may explore the cocoa and banana plantations in the Mamiku Gardens, which are on the island's eastern side. In addition to a diverse range of birds and insects, the gardens are home to an abundance of vibrant blooms. The Diamond Falls Botanical Garden has a café, mineral baths, and a cascade rich in minerals that is a favorite location for photographs.

14. Go to the Soufriere Region

There are a lot of things to do in the Soufrière region of Saint Lucia. Explore the town itself first, where you can browse the roadside shops for local handicrafts, see historical landmarks like the Church of the Assumption of the Blessed Virgin Mary, and enjoy views of the Pitons.

For those seeking a slower pace, the Anse Mamin beach is a great option. Adventurers may take up the Gros Piton Nature Trail or the Petit Piton Trail. The Tet Paul Nature Trail and Sulphur Springs Park are great places for nature enthusiasts to explore.

Make sure to stop at the viewpoint on the main road leading to Vieux Fort for a stunning view of the bay. Return to the beach after a long day of touring, unwind, and have a delicious creole meal.

15. Enjoy the Beaches' Magnificence

A well-known feature of Saint Lucia is its immaculate beaches. Thanks to its gentle winds from the Atlantic and Caribbean Seas, Sandy Beach on the southern end of the island is one of the greatest places to sunbathe.

Popular and family-friendly Reduit Beach is the ideal place to go sailing and snorkeling. Gorgeous palm trees and golden sand that meets blue seas may be seen at La Toc Beach. Grande Anse Beach is a fantastic location for romantic picnics, while Marigot Bay is a charming place with a number of little beaches that are ideal for some alone time.

16. Enjoy the Scene of Arts and Crafts
It's quite fantastic to explore Saint Lucia's art and craft culture. A large variety of regional specialties and spices, along with handcrafted goods like coconut candy, creole spice mixes, and mango passion rum sauce, can be found at the Castries food and craft market.

A craft brewery with a selection of specialty beers, including fig banana ale, rum barrel IPA, and passionfruit ale, is located close by. There's a beer garden at the neighboring Pointe Seraphine where guests may take in views of sailboats and live music. The Castries Market is the place to go if you want souvenirs. In addition to native spices and handcrafted soaps, you can discover a fantastic selection of trinkets and souvenirs here that will serve as a wonderful reminder of your trip to Saint Lucia.

17. Take up sport deep-sea fishing.
In Saint Lucia, deep sea sport fishing is a well-liked pastime, and the greatest spots are just two miles offshore. Deep sea fishing excursions in Saint Lucia often yield large game fish, including blue marlin, sailfish, yellowfin tuna, wahoo, and dorado. There are fishing charters available in the major places; however, be careful to verify reviews and make your reservation via a reliable provider.

IDEAL TIP: If you've never been on a fishing boat before, you should be aware that they move about a lot and may make you feel ill to your stomach. As a natural treatment for motion sickness, we take ginger tablets. Pharmacies sell these, or you can simply create a strong ginger tea. Because over-the-counter medications make me drowsy, I avoid using them.

18. See the Ponds and Waterfalls

Everybody should make time to see Saint Lucia's ponds and waterfalls. There is something for everyone, from the renowned Diamond Falls Waterfall and Mineral Baths & Spa to the more private Anse La Raye Waterfalls and La Tille Waterfall and Gardens.

You can see the 45-foot-tall, rainbow-colored waterfall at Diamond Falls, which is adorned with minerals. You may find a tranquil area with tumbling waterfalls, bamboo buildings, and a fish pond at the LaTille Falls and Garden. At Toraille Waterfall, you can cool down in the pool located at the foot of the waterfall. Although first rather frigid, the pool under the

Toraille Waterfall is beneficial to your health. Wearing water shoes is a good idea since it's also rather rough.

Another fantastic hike to check out is the Enbas Saut Waterfall hike in the Edmund Rain Forest Preserve. Wear appropriate hiking shoes since the trek involves many steep stairs and takes around two and a half hours. You'll be rewarded with a revitalizing swim in the cool waters after your hike.

Not to be missed is a scene from Superman II (1980) that was filmed at the Superman Falls, which is close to Soufrière.

19. Visit Pigeon Island National Park
Discover the history of the island's colonial past and take in the breathtaking vistas of Martinique on a tour to Pigeon Island National

Park in Saint Lucia. This park is well-liked because it offers access to private beaches, hiking paths, and birding opportunities.

Highlights of the trip include seeing the amazing 360-degree views from the fort, viewing the historic remains of Fort Rodney, and visiting a hilltop lookout with antique cannons and other relics. Additionally, you may investigate the little museum that has artifacts from World War II and military engagements between France and Britain. The park was used as a U.S. Station of Signals.

You may join a Sea Trek or SNUBA excursion, dine at the park's restaurants, and unwind on the two private beaches after seeing the sites.

20. Gain Knowledge of the Brewing Industry

Nothing beats a refreshing beer on a hot day, but did you know that the island is home to a sizable brewery? There are a lot of things to do and see when you visit the Antillia Brewing Company in Saint Lucia. You may try some of their most well-liked beverages, such as a rum cask IPA, an imperial chocolate stout, and a passionfruit ale, at Point Seraphine, which is close to center Castries.

There could also be seasonal offerings available, such as fig banana ale. You may eat spicy jerk wings, hotdogs, burgers, and more while sipping the local craft beer, enjoying live music, or gazing at the sailboats docked in the port.

In addition, the region offers lectures and workshops, outdoor activities, sightseeing cruises, excursions, and other unique experiences.

21. Discover the Hiking Trails in the Rainforest

Discovering the vast richness of nature may be greatly enhanced by hiking in Saint Lucia's rainforest. The Barre de l'Isle Rain Forest Trail in Castries, the Tet Paul Nature Trail close to the hamlet of Soufriere, and the Enbas Saut Waterfall Trail in the Edmund Rainforest Preserve are the most well-liked routes to explore.

The Enbas Saut Waterfall Trail is a more difficult hike that takes around two and a half hours and needs sturdy hiking shoes because of its steep terrain. It takes around 45 minutes to complete the intermediate Tet Paul Nature Trail. Awe-inspiring 360-degree views await you at the summit, with clear days revealing the nearby islands of Martinique and St. Vincent.

Enjoy breathtaking vistas on an easy stroll along the Barre de l'Isle Rain Forest Trail. Additionally, you may take a three- or four-hour guided tour of the Edmund Forest Reserve with authorization from the Forestry Department.

22. Visit the Farm of Butterflies

The breathtaking beauty and educational opportunities of Saint Lucia's Butterfly Farm make it a well-liked tourist destination. The farm, which located in Soufriere, is home to many different types of tropical plants, birds, and other animals in addition to a broad range of local and migratory butterflies.

You may enjoy a guided tour of the farm to discover more about the native plants and animals as well as the butterfly's life cycle. The

Butterfly Farm also provides a unique chance to see the butterflies' color changes as they become older, in addition to a huge range of kid-friendly crafts and activities.

23. Scale Petit Piton

An amazing experience is climbing Petit Piton. It's a difficult climb due to the rocky terrain and steep slopes, but the view is breathtaking from the summit. You will see the island's rich and colorful foliage as you climb, and you may even get a sight of the azure Caribbean Sea.

The expansive vista of the island awaits you at the peak, making the effort worthwhile. When the weather is clear, you can see for kilometers and enjoy the island's splendor from an entirely new angle. Climbing Petit Piton is an unforgettable experience that may be achieved with the appropriate guidance and a little perseverance.

Its sibling, Gros Piton, offers a longer and higher trek if you're seeking for something even more difficult.

24. Ride a horse on Cas En Bas Beach.

It's a unique experience in and of itself to visit Cas En Bas Beach in Saint Lucia. It is elevated to a whole new level when done on a horse. This is a well-liked pastime that lets you explore the beach and surroundings. You may go on guided excursions with Sandy Hoofs St. Lucia or Atlantic Shores Riding Stables, and your guide will show you the finest places to go and assist you in developing a stronger relationship with your horse.

As you ride your horse down the sandy beach and bathe in the surf, take in the beauty of the surroundings. A breathtaking background for your journey is provided by the neighboring mountains, banana plantation, and Atlantic shoreline.

25. Take a Therapeutic Mud Bath

Taking a therapeutic mud bath entails drawing minerals and other healthy substances from mud that is made of clay. Because the mud, sulfur, and hot spring water in this kind of bath assist lessen tension, discomfort, and inflammation, it is well recognized to offer therapeutic benefits. Additionally, it may aid in bodily detoxification, circulation enhancement, and texture and look improvement of the skin.

With so many volcanoes and hot springs, Saint Lucia is the ideal destination for a healing mud bath. The volcanic mud and warm water of the nearby Sulphur Springs are well recognized for their therapeutic properties.

This mud is said to help mend and relax sore muscles after travel, decrease inflammation, and make you appear ten years younger. It's a terrific way to unwind after a long day of touring since the mixture of mud, sulfur, and hot spring water helps to soothe the body and mind.

Explore the well-known Pitons, a UNESCO World Heritage Site, first. After that, cool down from the tropical heat by swimming on one of the many beaches or waterfalls on the island. Visit Soufriere, the only drive-in volcano in the world, for a once-in-a-lifetime adventure.

The primary draw of Saint Lucia is the natural world. Take a zip line trip under the canopy or go hiking into the jungle if you're feeling very daring. In order to see the colorful marine life, you may also go diving a few miles offshore or snorkel in the shallow waters along the beach.

Consider going on a sightseeing boat around St. Lucia for a more laid-back experience. A romantic sunset cruise or a spa treatment are additional options offered by some of the establishments. With so many public beaches to choose from, including Reduit Beach, Anse de Pitons, Anse Cochon, Anse de Sables, and Labas Beach, beach hopping is undoubtedly one of the best things to do in St. Lucia.

Which attractions are popular in St. Lucia?

The Pitons, the magnificent twin volcanic peaks of St. Lucia, may be visited by foot, ATV, or helicopter. The island's undulating terrain makes Sulphur Springs Park and hiking and off-road adventures ideal. There are many charming beaches, bays, fishing communities, and coral reefs for diving and snorkeling along the breathtaking coastline.

Aerial tramway, zip lines, rum tastings, guided city walks, Pigeon Island National Park, Gros Piton Nature Trail, and Castries with its bustling market are among the other attractions. Other well-liked sports on the island include ATVing through the jungle and horseback riding.

Chapter 6: St. Lucian Cuisine

Local Dishes and Flavors

A little island in the Caribbean's Lesser Antilles is called St. Lucia. There are nearly 700 islands in the Caribbean, all of which are part of sovereign states, however they are all situated in the Atlantic Ocean. There are twenty-one more dependent nations. The island of Martinique, which is visible on a clear day, is closest to St. Lucia.

Although tourism is its primary economy, it has a long history of exporting bananas to nations like the UK. The rainy and dry seasons alternate. Most days of the year, the temperature is in the 80s. The nation is home to the only drive-in volcano in the world and has very steep terrain with a beautiful rainforest in the heart of the island.

In St. Lucia, English is the official language, but Kweyol, often known as St. Lucian Creole, is the traditional tongue.

Most Well-liked St. Lucian Dishes
The staples of traditional St. Lucian cuisine include meat, fish, spices, and ground supplies. It is influenced by British, French, African, and Indian cuisines. Vegetables that grow underground, such as yams and other root vegetables, are considered ground supplies.

Near the island's coast are a large number of fishing settlements. Seafood abounds, including yellow tuna, snapper, conch, lobster, and octopus. Although grilling over an open flame is the traditional way, St Lucia has seen a rise in the popularity of barbecue in recent decades.

1. Green Figs and Saltfish

Fish and bananas make up green figs and saltfish. Unripe green bananas are called green figs. Salted water is used to boil them. Cod fish that has been salted and dried is called saltfish, and it doesn't need to be refrigerated. The salted fish is cooked, then stewed with onions and spices after being washed multiple times to remove the majority of the salt.

Saint Lucians have a particular place in their hearts for saltfish and green figs. This is a typical dinner to prepare at home, but it's also served in restaurants. It may be eaten on its own or combined with a number of other traditional dishes, such as cucumber salad or ground supplies. Cucumber salad is made using grated or sliced cucumbers, salt, and occasionally other flavorings like oil and garlic. In St. Lucia, this side is quite prevalent.

2. Chicken Backs

This is a chicken meal that has been stewed. Backs are the leftovers from a chicken that have had its legs, wings, and breasts removed. The bird's back bone and any remaining bits of flesh are still connected. You may serve stewed backs with any kind of starch, but the most common is green figs. The poorest people who couldn't afford the more expensive cuts of beef used to appreciate this meal.

3. Green Fig Salad

A salad made with green bananas, salt fish, mayonnaise, and flavorings is called green fig salad. After boiling, the green bananas are chilled. The cooked saltfish, mayonnaise, onions, garlic, green onions, spice peppers, salt, and black pepper are then combined with the pieces after being sliced into tiny dice.

Before serving, refrigerate the salad. Carrots and green beans or peas are sometimes added to green fig salad in St. Lucia, however it's up for debate whether they are necessary. The people who reside in Castries, the capital of the island, are more likely to do this.

4. Hot Bakes and Cocoa Tea

Cocoa tea is a beverage consisting only of cocoa, while hot bakes are fried flatbreads. Although there are other methods to prepare baked goods, the most fundamental dough consists of wheat flour, water, baking powder, and salt. Butter, sugar, and yeast are optional components.

A big ball of dough is divided into smaller pieces, shaped into balls, pressed into the shape of a disc, and deep-fried till golden. Because to the modest puffiness, filling and slicing are made easier. Although it may be filled with anything, the most popular filling is stewed saltfish.

The tropical plant used to make chocolate is called cocoa. The paste made from pulverized cocoa nibs is shaped into little logs and dried, resulting in what are known as cocoa sticks.

When ready to use, the solid cocoa stick is shredded and boiled with spices like nutmeg, cinnamon, and bay leaves in boiling water. Depending on how much spice was used, the addition of milk and sugar results in a rich, sweet chocolate beverage with a hint of spice.

Coco tea and hot bakes are a match made in heaven. It's a favorite dish on rainy days.

5. Dumplings

St. Lucian dumplings are usually cooked in soup or broth, and dumplings are simply cooked bits of dough. The dumplings come in a variety of sizes and forms, from quarter-sized balls to enormous flat dumplings that are often cooked for community events. Because the latter kind of dumpling is more filling, it incorporates cornmeal.

6. Bouyon

The ingredients for bouyon include salted pork, beans, veggies, and dumplings. It is a thick, chunky soup. Salted pig tails with red beans and dumplings are the most often consumed kind. In some dishes, coconut milk is included together with other meats like chicken and lamb.

The term "bouyon" is derived from the French word "bouillon," which meaning broth, often prepared by stewing vegetables, fish, or meat.

7. Smoked Herrings with Breadfruit

This is a meal that has boiled or roasted breadfruit with stewed fish. Another fish that doesn't need to be refrigerated is herring, which is dried and smoked over an open flame. Before being stewed with onions, the smoked herring is first boiled and deboned.

The huge, starchy breadfruit fruit grows on a tree that is similarly big in size. When mature, the starches turn into sugar, making it delicious and almost pillowy soft. You may eat it uncooked. Breadfruit is hard to consume raw; it has to be cooked. Typically, it is sliced and fried, roasted whole, or peeled and split into smaller pieces for boiling. Because the meal tends to be a touch dry, the stewed herrings are placed on top of the baked breadfruit and sometimes drizzled with a little oil. Cucumber salad is often served with it.

8. Paime

The best way to describe pâte is as a boiling cake. It is quite different from tamales, yet it has certain similarities. Cornmeal, sugar, coconut shreds, pumpkin or sweet potatoes, cinnamon, and nutmeg make up the essential components. After being cooked until soft, the pumpkin is mashed and combined with the other ingredients. Spooned onto banana leaf, the mixture is sealed with a knot. The sealed packages are heated in steaming water until solid.

On Jounen Kweyol, also known as Creole Day, in October, traditional cuisine are honored. Because of its immense popularity, October is now recognized as Creole Heritage Month, during which the residents spend their weekends visiting various towns and events on the island and indulging in regional cuisine and libations. Paime is offered by street sellers and is generally available throughout this month.

9. Lambi

Conch flesh is called lambi. It may be made in a number of methods. Conch is fried or grilled after being spiced. Making a stew out of the lambi is an additional technique.

This dish is a favorite during fish fries, also referred to as seafood fiestas. At night, the fishing communities throw feasts during which they cook a wide variety of newly caught seafood.

10. Accra

Fish cakes, or accra, are saltfish fritters. Finely shredded saltfish, flour, water, and spices are used in its preparation. After being scooped into heated oil, the batter is cooked. Typically, it is consumed as a snack. Accra was traditionally made for Easter, a time when people abstain from eating meat.

11. Cassava Bread

Yucca, sometimes referred to as cassava root, is used to make this kind of unleavened bread. All you need for the dish is cassava flour, water, and salt. After shaping the mixture into discs, it is fried over a hot cast iron. Despite being a basic dish, this one isn't often encountered in homes due to its difficulty of preparation.

Cassava bread is available in the early-morning markets or from street sellers that visit different villages and knock on people's doors. Flavors of cassava bread that are more recent include chocolate, cinnamon, apple, cherry, and saltfish.

12. Fish Broth

The ingredients of St. Lucian fish broth include fish, green bananas, ground pork, various vegetables, including carrots, and a variety of spices. The broths often use whatever is in season, and the recipes vary. The fish and veggies are cooked in the broth until they are soft. Unlike fish soup from Trinidad, this broth is often devoid of spicy peppers.

13. Dhal

Dhal is fried bread that is filled. Baking powder, salt, water, and flour are combined to make the dough. After rolling it into a circle, one side is stuffed with filling. The empty side is pinched shut after being folded over into the form of a half moon. Next, it's fried. The most popular fillings are stewed saltfish and curry split peas.

Popular Restaurants

Excellent dining establishments in St. Lucia make the most of the island's reputation as a gourmet haven. Whether you're looking for a seat amid the trees or a bite to eat by the coast, the location is unmatched. The sounds of the Caribbean, from the finest local singers to the melodies of nature, provide the ideal setting.

Most of the best restaurants provide fresh seafood and Creole food, with a few foreign menu items for a little flavor of home. You will have an abundance of options during your journey to St. Lucia as chefs from all over the Caribbean flock to establish their restaurants there. We've compiled a list of the best restaurants in St. Lucia that we think you should try.

1. Pink Plantation House

In St. Lucia, the Pink Plantation House is a Creole restaurant with a view of Castries. For photographers, the home and art gallery are worth a visit. You will think you have traveled back in time when you see the pink, wooden colonial home tucked away in the grounds.

Highlight of the property is the restaurant, which serves Creole food made using local ingredients. The Pink House salad made with saltfish and grilled fish are very good. To secure a seat on the veranda for brunch, we advise making a reservation in advance. The delightful, delicate fragrances of the nearby plantation will greet you.

Location: Chef Harry Drive, Morne Fortune, Castries, St. Lucia

Open: Daily from 10 am to 3 pm

2. Naked Fisherman Restaurant

Beneath Cap Maison in St Lucia, Naked Fisherman Restaurant is a laid-back bar and grill joint. Situated in a protected cove, it provides sweeping views of the Caribbean Sea. A decent selection of appetizers, entrees, and BBQ platters are available (after 6 pm).

Naked Fisherman Restaurant specializes on seafood, as you would expect, and their menu features freshly caught fish every day. Yellowfin tuna, snow crab, and spiny lobster are all offered with regional sides such Caribbean slaw and caramelized plantain. Every evening, the venue has a true Caribbean flavor thanks to regular DJs.

Location: Smugglers Cove Road Gros Islet, St. Lucia

Open: Friday from 9 am to 5 pm, Saturday–Thursday from 9 am to 10 pm

3. Rabot Restaurant by Hotel Chocolat

Located in St. Lucia on a verdant, sustainable cocoa plantation, is Hotel Chocolat's Rabot Restaurant. Even while cacao is used in all foods, not all of them are sweet; in fact, this ingredient from the Caribbean often gives savory foods a deep flavor.

Raw cacao is used to marinade steaks, fresh cacao nibs are used to garnish salads, and tart cacao pulp adds flavor to drinks. Desserts are a must-try, particularly the chocolate lava at Rabot Restaurant. Find out more about the "Tree to Bar" experience, which includes a tour of the cacao groves, cacao picking, and chocolate bar making.

Location: LC Soufriere, St. Lucia
Open: Daily from 7 am to 9.30 pm

4. Rum Cave

A little eatery called The Rum Cave is situated at the edge of Marigot Bay. Its air-conditioned interior may be used for dining, but the nicest tables are those by the ocean, where you can hear the sound of the waves crashing on the decks. At night, the beautiful atmosphere is enhanced by live music and the illumination of docked boats.

Try the conch Bolognese dish at The Rum Cave, which serves fusion cuisine as well as regional specialties like St. Lucian fish soup. Get the famous Chocolaté Fondu for a dessert that is really unparalleled.

Location: XX7G+QWV, St. Lucia
Open: Daily from 10 am to 11 pm

5. Julietta's

With its elevated location above Marigot Bay, Julietta's provides breathtaking views of the Caribbean Sea. If you want to go straight to the cuisine, you may arrange for a shuttle or make the hike up the hill on foot.

Julietta's serves up delicious, reasonably priced island cuisine that is presented in a fine-dining manner. Salads and freshly caught seafood are two of the restaurant's specialties. You'll be treated to international favorites like shakshuka, fresh burrata, and a selection of French croque dishes if you can make there for breakfast.

Location: Castries, St. Lucia
Open: Monday–Thursday and Saturday from 9 am to 10 pm (closed on Fridays and Sundays)

6. Orlando's

Orlando's is a modest farm-to-table eatery located in Soufrière's downtown. It takes great satisfaction in using fresh products from nearby sustainable farms. You will be given a personalized experience, as the amiable proprietor is pleased to walk you through the preparation of each meal.

The five-course tasting menu has meals cooked using fresh mangoes, blackeye beans, and sugarcane that are cultivated nearby. It is refreshed on a regular basis. There's rum pairings available as well. Orlando wants to provide you with an experience rather than simply a meal.

Location: Bridge St, St. Lucia

Open: Tuesday from 7.30 am to 10 am and from 2 pm to 9 pm, Wednesday–Monday from 7.30 am to 10 am and from noon to 9 pm

7. The Coal Pot

The Coal Pot is a waterfront eatery located in Castries, a short distance from the cruise liner terminal, with a view of Vigie Marina. The Coal Pot, which gets its name from traditional Caribbean cooking techniques, offers some of the greatest seafood on the island by combining contemporary fine dining with heritage.

Utilizing the daily catches to the fullest, the cuisine is always changing. Alongside pita pockets, local favorites like saltfish salad and calamari Creole are served. There's usually a variety of steak cuts on the grill menu. Try it if you're in St. Lucia during lobster season; it's delicious. It is made using time-honored techniques that have been passed down through the centuries.

Location: Seraphine Road, Castries 00124, St. Lucia

Open: Monday from noon to 3 pm and from 5.30 pm to 7 pm, Tuesday–Saturday from noon to 3 pm and from 6.30 to 9.30 pm (closed on Sundays)

8. Treehouse at Anse Chastanet

Treehouse at Anse Chastanet allows you eat amid tropical trees, owing to its placement under a forest canopy. The restaurant's vast cuisine, which includes fresh daily catches, marlin, and seared scallops prepared in the Caribbean way, perfectly complements its stunning surroundings. For those who prefer to go outside, there is an Indian cuisine as well.

For most customers, the breakfast is a highlight. Above the trees, you may have a traditional American breakfast while taking in the expansive views that are enhanced by the early wind. You may then go over to Anse Chastanet Beach to go snorkeling and swimming.

Location: 1 Anse Chastanet Road, Soufriere, St. Lucia
Open: Monday–Saturday from 10 am to 9.30 pm, Sunday from noon to 9 pm

9. Dasheene at Ladera Resort

Luxurious dining establishment Dasheene at Ladera provides breathtaking views of Petit Piton Point and the Caribbean Sea. Situated above Soufrière, a UNESCO World Heritage site in St Lucia, it is part of an opulent resort.

Though the menu changes periodically, local fishermen's St Lucian seafood is always available. The coconut salad and pan-seared kingfish are very good. If you want to spoil your special someone, Dasheene also offers a honeymoon meal. The corner table on the terrace is the most romantic place in the restaurant, so be sure you reserve it in advance.

Location: Rabot Estate Soufriere Post Office, Jalousle, St. Lucia

Open: Daily from 7 am to 10 pm

10. Bayside Restaurant

In addition to serving international cuisine, Bayside Restaurant offers freshly caught seafood from the Caribbean. It is situated under Petit Piton Point and offers breathtaking views of St. Lucia's Jalousie Bay. It's a remarkably picture-perfect view, and you can see Jalousie Dock trawlers coming and going.

With daily catches keeping the cuisine as fresh as the fish, the seafood is excellent. A delicious French cuisine including items like confit duck and cordon bleu is also available. In the opulent Sugar Beach, A Viceroy Resort, sits the Bayside Restaurant.

Location: Val Des Pitons Forbidden Beach, La Baie de Silence Soufrière, St. Lucia

Open: Daily from 12.30 pm to 3 pm and from 6 pm to 10 pm

Chapter 7: Nightlife and Entertainment

Bars and Clubs

The Greatest Bars in Saint Lucia

The white-sand beaches and steaming tropical rainforests of St. Lucia, a Caribbean paradise, may be its most well-known features, but the islanders also enjoy a good night out. Here's my suggestion for the greatest spots to get both the best views and the tastiest beverages.

Gros Islet has been hosting a weekly street celebration for over 50 years, and you can always find a refreshing Piton beer, named after the mountain range in St. Lucia, or a rum drink nearby.

Gros Islet Street Party

The Gros Islet jump up is the greatest location to party on the island, even though it's not really a bar. Every Friday starting at dusk, locals set up tables in the street and blast reggae music on the sound system to kick off the festivities. Freshly caught lobster and conch, sizzling hot chicken, and tabletop beers with a kick are all served by barbecues, while local arts and crafts are sold by vendors.

Boardwalk Bar

Make sure to arrive well in advance to see the breathtaking sunsets from this unassuming pub situated just by the marina in Rodney Bay. Not only is this relaxed pub a favorite spot for boat arrivals, but locals adore coming here for happy hour after work. Families are invited to relax and have a beverage while listening to live music on the weekends.

Roots Beach Bar

This vividly colored wooden cabin, painted in the distinctive Rastafarian hues of red, green, and yellow, is easily seen from Las Bas Beach in Marigot Bay. With your toes on the sand and a nice drink in hand, enjoy the seaside vistas and the aroma of spicy chicken roasting over a charcoal barbecue. Elevated palm trees canopy above shade the Caribbean heat, or take a seat at the counter to engage in conversation with proprietors Sue and Peter, often known as Fluffy and Wilfred.

Cane Bar

Although it's not the most affordable place to drink on the island, rum fans shouldn't pass up a night at Sugar Beach - a Viceroy Resort's ultra-chic rum bar. A trained rumologist is there to assist you with your selections, and a selection of the best-aged spirits in the world are readily available, coupled with an outstanding cocktail list. We suggest the hot chili passion, a rum concoction of ginger, cranberries, passionfruit, and chili.

Rehab

The rehab facility bears the name of the late Amy Winehouse, a legendary musician who fell in love with St. Lucia so strongly that she spent many months there on vacation. Rehab, located in the center of Rodney Bay Village, is a terrific spot for drinks, people watching, and Motown music. The crowd is lively and the establishment has a nice vibe. Start here to ensure entrance before heading to the many pubs and clubs along Rodney Bay's strip.

Coastline Beach Bar

This outdoor pub in Vieux Fort offers cool drinks and breathtaking views of the sea if you can't bear to leave the beach. A limited menu of regional cuisine and an extensive variety of rum are available at this all-day beachside tavern, which is especially popular on weekends. If you're very bold on a Friday night, you can even participate in karaoke.

Coconutz Bar and Grill

Hiding behind a parking lot, Coconutz is the liveliest place in Rodney Bay and is a dependable choice for those seeking late evenings, inexpensive cocktails, and loud music. It's best to arrive early and stuff yourself with the fairly priced tacos from the bar before the party really gets going, since it becomes extremely packed after 10pm. Open till two in the morning on Fridays and Saturdays, but

Tuesdays are when the smart people go since drinks are just $1 on that day.

Rhumba Daiquiri Grill and Bar

If you're going to the renowned Gros Islet street party on a Friday night, start the evening here and fill up on the tastiest jerk chicken in town beforehand. Drinks from the bar, such as tropical daiquiris that taste like the Caribbean when poured over ice, go well with the freshly cooked barbecued food. The rum drink is really potent, so beware.

Spinnakers Beach Bar

This unpretentious pub near Reduit Beach's northern end loves to get things going early, opening daily in time for breakfast. Swimmers, day-trippers from cruise ships, and boaters visit for lunch and dinner, but the ideal time to visit is around 5 p.m., when the bar has a daily happy hour with two-for-one drinks and a fun vibe. Try a classic martini or order a piton snow, which consists of crushed ice, rum, lime juice, and coconut cream.

Naked Fisherman

This beach bar isn't as wicked as it sounds, so don't worry. It is said to have been called after the three fisherman who used to come here every morning to swim in the buff when the Cap Maison resort was being constructed. Although they are no longer there, the atmosphere is still laid-back, complete with wooden deck chairs for lounging on the beach, free water activities, live music, and what are maybe the tastiest burgers on the island.

Live Music and Events

Top 10 Most Well-Known Celebrations in Saint Lucia

The festivals on this Caribbean island, with its rich heritage and lively culture, provide great street food, live music, and a festive vibe. It's easy to fit in at least one of the year-round events on the following list while visiting St. Lucia. To help you plan your trip, we've compiled a list of some of Saint Lucia's most well-known events.

1. Jazz Festival in Saint Lucia

The Saint Lucia Jazz Festival has developed into one of the most anticipated Caribbean events of the year and one of the most significant national gatherings.

The yearly Saint Lucia Jazz Festival attracts bass guitars, trumpets, and saxophones from well-known artists to the Caribbean island. Every year, as May comes near, Saint Lucia Jazz attracts attention from all around the globe as people eagerly await the reveal of the regularly scheduled roster, which features a star-studded cast. In past lineups, bassist Christian McBride, trumpeter Etienne Charles, and R&B and jazz vocalist Ledisi have all played.

The multi-day event, which is produced in collaboration with Jazz at Lincoln Center, serves as a focal point for festivals, educational initiatives, and concerts. You have plenty of opportunities to dance to the music since it's hosted at several sites across the island.

Month: May
Location: Various locations

2. Feast of Fishermen

Fishermen's Feast is one of Saint Lucia's most well-known celebrations. Like Americans celebrate Thanksgiving, the fishermen of St. Lucia celebrate this annual event on the last Sunday in June. The intricately decorated boats are traditionally blessed after an early morning service. It's colorful and significant to the local fishermen. Cooperatives of fishermen on the islands worked together to organize this celebration. While each one is running its own activities concurrently, they all start with a church service before moving on to meals, parties, and other forms of entertainment.

This holiday is one of the most important ones for fishermen since it gives them a chance to give thanks for another successful year of catching a lot of fish. Enjoy delectable food at communal dinners, see people dressed to the nines for church services, and see fishing boats blessed all over the coast to celebrate Fishermen's Feast.

Month: June

Location: All along St Lucia

3. Carnival in Saint Lucia

The most popular event on the island is the monthly Saint Lucia Carnival, which is a month-long celebration and mash-up of Saint Lucian art, culture, music, and dance.

The Saint Lucian Carnival festivities come to an end with the carnival parade. Among the titles previously selected are Carnival Queen, Calypso Monarch, Panorama Champions, and Party Monarch. Bands vie for the coveted title of "Band of the Year" during Carnival Monday and Tuesday, which are a riot of color and melody.

The carnival's jam-packed schedule, which includes J'ouvert street parties, boat rides, music, and more, culminates with a two-day parade. Live bands and DJs offer the music, which is a celebration of Caribbean culture that locals and costumed dancers move to.

Month: July and June
Location: Pigeon Point and further locations

4. Mercury Festival

Mercury Fest, one of the most well-known events in Saint Lucia, is a fantastic summertime highlight and is regarded as one of the best beach parties in the Caribbean. With hundreds of boats coming from Martinique, Guadalupe, St. Vincent, Barbados, and Trinidad, it's a party in paradise.

The Mercury Fest celebration is an exclusive event focused on offering a distinctive beach experience, not just a beach party. Both locals and tourists will enjoy delectable local brews and beverages, excellent food, and nonstop entertainment. Along with local and regional artists, dance until your feet ache to the sounds of the best French DJs.

As the event becomes bigger and more popular, the variety of attendees rises. Barbados, Trinidad, Martinique, and Guadeloupe are no longer the sole places tourists go. Visitors from France, Africa, Canada, and Puerto Rico have flocked to this historic event.

When: Summer
Location: Pigeon Island Beach

5. Roots and Soul

The three-day Roots & Soul festival in St Lucia will include performances, master classes, and meetings between artists and other musicians, all devoted to celebrating performers who are pushing the boundaries of reggae, conscious hip-hop, Afropunk, and R&B. There will be both free and paid performances across the island, similar to Saint Lucia Jazz, culminating at the Pigeon Island National Landmark. One of Saint Lucia's most well-known celebrations is this one.

On Pigeon Island, the main stage has hosted performances like UB40, Lee John, Mya, and Ginuwine in the past. Check out St. Lucia's official website to find out who is performing this year.

While some of these live concerts are completely free to attend, others have a price and need advance booking.

Month: August

Location: Pigeon Island.

6. Creole Heritage Month

Discover St. Lucia's rich cultural, ethnic, and artistic past via music, art, food, and more during this month-long festival. Four townships or towns are selected year to host the festivities, so as the day draws near, keep a look out for further details.

During Creole Heritage Month, you can expect to see authentic Creole cuisine at many resorts and restaurants, as well as colorful madras cloth used by the island's people as decorations and for storytelling dances and performances in public spaces.

On the last Sunday in October, which is Jounen Kwéyl, a day honoring the heritage of the island, Creole Heritage Month comes to an end.

Make it a point to visit, sample some of the delicious, original St. Lucian food, and join in the procession to dance the night away. It's a great chance to enjoy yourself and discover more about St. Lucia's past.

Month: October

Location: All along St Lucia

7. Saint Lucia Food & Rum Festival

Over the course of three days, the Saint Lucia Food and Rum Festival showcases the best of the island's culinary and rum heritage. The Food & Rum Festival is a gastronomic extravaganza that attracts world-class chefs, connoisseurs of rum, food reviewers, and gourmands from outside the Caribbean. A number of renowned chefs create meals that draw inspiration from the unique cuisine of the island, which blends elements of Indian,

African, British, and French cuisines. A festival featuring internationally recognized Caribbean food and beverage experts and custom-made dishes that will transform your understanding of Caribbean cuisine.

Dinners prepared by our guest chefs, rum lectures, chef demos, rum tastings including more than 40 rums from the area, and entertainment on Saturday and Sunday evenings are all part of the Festival schedule.

Month: September
Location: All along St Lucia

8. Wellness Music Festival
At the health Music Festival, which blends music with health, nourish your mind, body, and spirit! Anyone who wants to take advantage of the added benefits of wellness-specific

activities in addition to the "relaxing and renewing power of music" could attend the new Wellness Music Festival in St. Lucia. Intimate performances will be led by three-time Grammy and Tony Award-winning jazz performer Dee Dee Bridgewater.

This environmentally conscious festival will kick out at one of the best wellness resorts in the world, BodyHoliday, and include a range of holistic practitioners, nutritionists, yoga instructors, and others who are keen to offer their tips for leading better lives. One of the most well-known events in Saint Lucia is the Wellness Music Festival.

Of course, music plays a big role in this festival. Scheduled to perform are a range of international, regional, and local artists who all support a healthy living.

Month: September

Location: Pigeon Island.

9. Festival of Lights

On December 13, National Day, and the Feast of Saint Luce, Patron Saint of Light, the Festival of Lights takes place. The occasion honors the victory of good over evil, the rebirth of life, and light over darkness. The first week of December sees a grand Lantern Competition to kick off the celebrations.

People gather around St. Lucia to celebrate the victory of light over darkness with a stunning display of lanterns and fireworks on this occasion that you won't soon forget. A beautiful lantern competition takes place in the first week of December, and on December 12th there's a parade that doubles as a joyous celebration and Christmas entertainment.

During the Festival of Lights, guests will recall being enthralled with the breathtaking illuminated exhibits, vibrant ambiance, and exceptional St Lucian customs and history that are being showcased.

Month: December
Location: All along St Lucia

10. Atlantic Rally for Cruisers

The biennial transatlantic sailing event for cruiser boats has been called the Atlantic Rally for Cruisers (ARC) since 1986. There is also a sailing race included. ARC takes place in Las Palmas de Gran Canaria in late November and ends at Rodney Bay, Saint Lucia, in the Caribbean, just before Christmas.

The world's biggest transoceanic sailing race takes place every year, with approximately 200 ships making the journey from Gran Canaria to Saint Lucia. After two or three weeks, the sailors arrive at Rodney Bay Marina, where music and festivities await them on their 2,700 nautical mile voyage. There's rum punch, fresh fruit, and cool beer waiting for every boat. Whenever you arrive, day or night, the welcome party will be there to greet you! Due to the abundance of activities and the kind hospitality of Saint Lucians, a lot of yachts choose to spend Christmas on the island.

Month: November to December

Cultural Shows

Through a variety of cultural performances and events that highlight the island's history, music, dance, and customs, you may get a taste of St. Lucia's rich cultural legacy. You may take in the following cultural performances and activities while visiting St. Lucia:

La Rose and La Marguerite Festivals: These are the two biggest cultural events in St. Lucia. La Marguerite honors the marguerite blossom, whereas La Rose honors the rose. These celebrations honor the island's African and French ancestry with vibrant processions, traditional dances, and entertainment.

Anse La Raye Seafood Friday: This weekly event in the fishing town of Anse La Raye provides an insight into local culture, even if it's not a conventional cultural presentation. You may take in the vibrant ambiance of a Caribbean fish fry, local cuisine, and live music.

Cultural Dance Performances: Cultural dance shows are held at a few St. Lucian hotels and resorts. These performances often include traditional dances like bele, quadrille, and other Creole dances, giving guests a genuine cultural experience.

Fond Latisab Creole Park: This cultural park, which is situated in Anse La Raye, provides a unique chance to engage with Creole culture. It includes artisan workshops, traditional huts, and cultural exhibits such as traditional dance and music performances.

Street Performers: You will often encounter street performers and buskers exhibiting many facets of St. Lucian culture at tourist destinations like Castries and Rodney Bay, from music and dancing to arts and crafts.

Celebrations & Festivals: St. Lucia has a number of festivals and events with a cultural focus throughout the year. For instance, local performers and artists are often included at the St. Lucia Jazz Festival.

Local Art and Craft Markets: Local markets may introduce you to the arts and crafts of the island, even if they are not part of conventional cultural events. In addition to selling their goods, many craftsmen also provide talks or demonstrations of their trade.

Make careful to research the dates and venues of any cultural events or performances that could coincide with your trip to St. Lucia while making travel plans. These encounters give visitors a greater appreciation for St. Lucia's rich cultural history and its kind, hospitable populace.

Chapter 8: Shopping and Souvenirs

Local Crafts and Art

You most likely had visions of the Pitons, white sand beaches, and refreshing beverages under the sun when you planned your vacation to St. Lucia.

It's possible that the last thought on your mind was what you would carry home. We're here to assist, and we believe you should purchase some interesting art and craft items while visiting St. Lucia.

You will not only be assisting regional artists and craftspeople, but you will also be bringing home a real work of art that you may keep for a very long time.

1. Works of Art and Prints

Paintings and prints are among the greatest art items to buy in St. Lucia, whether you're looking for a distinctive memento or a present for someone back home.

There are many excellent visual artists on the island who produce stunning work. The majority of paintings in the area often highlight our stunning scenery, which includes the Pitons, beaches, and waterfalls.

Prints of these sceneries are often available in the Vendor's Arcade across from Castries Market.

Not only can St. Lucian artists paint breathtaking landscapes, but they also make abstract art and paintings that reflect the local nature and way of life.

You may find and buy paintings of this kind at the MeCurator Art Gallery in Massade, Gros Islet. Gilroy Hippolyte is one of the highlighted artists; the locals like his vibrant abstract paintings, which could find a new home with you.

Ron Henry, a well-known artist from the southern town of Choiseul, has had his work shown and purchased in the UK.

Henry has said that his paintings, which include people fishing, exploding bamboo, and hummingbirds, would be appreciated by everyone who enjoys traveling to the Caribbean.

There is a vast array of paintings available for selection when it comes to arts and crafts.

2. Wooden Statues

For Saint Lucians, wood has long been a valuable material—not only for building, but also for the craft industry.

Numerous local artists create wood carvings in a variety of styles and sizes, since they are highly sought-after.

You're certain to come across an artist selling wood carvings whether you're meandering around the Castries Market or stopping by for a brief look around.

These might be carved wooden kitchenware, bowls, or figurines with landscapes. Wooden carvings in smaller sizes are preferable since larger ones may make your luggage heavier when you go home.

Joseph Eudovic, a well-known wood sculptor in St. Lucia, runs Eudovic's Art Studio in Good Lands, Castries, where he creates his works.

There are tours offered to the studio where you can see Mr. Eudovic or his knowledgeable crew hone their technique and perhaps purchase a wood carving if you're interested in seeing this master sculptor in action.

Even while these sculptures may not be the cheapest available, you can be confident that you're getting a top-notch product from a well-known craftsman.

3. Locally Made Jewelry & Accessories

There have always been small-scale jewelers in St. Lucia; they can generally be found in the Vendor's Arcade, the Castries Market, street booths, and popular tourist destinations like the Sulphur Springs.

These items, which are often composed of beads and shells, frequently come in sets that include a bracelet, necklace, and earrings.

Some jewelry designs are starting to become more well-liked, even though they are still produced and purchased in large quantities. These days, copper jewelry with stones and crystal accents is highly fashionable.

One may acquire and bring home unique copper jewelry, which ranges in complexity from basic patterns to intricate showpiece pieces.

An indigenous firm called Bandbox uses patterned cloth to make versatile accessories. Moodcords, which are the pieces worn as necklaces, are available.

The good thing is that you can get these items anywhere in the globe, in case you forget to pack any fantastic accessories for your vacation to St. Lucia.

You're likely to find a variety of other jewelry alternatives and accessories, such coconut shell earrings, while touring Castries and popular perspectives in St. Lucia. These products often cost a few dollars and are excellent presents for your friends back home.

4. Straw Products

Creating a variety of goods out of straw and other grasses has long been a major aspect of St. Lucia's creative culture.

Over time, new styles have been added to this tradition as it has been handed down through the generations.

Typically, straw goods are created by selecting and classifying the proper grasses, then allowing them to dry in the sun until they become a light shade of brown.

After that, they are braided into a plethora of handcrafted items, such as bags, coasters, mats, baskets, and handbags. Typically, madras cloth and vibrantly colored embroidery are used to make purses and bags.

Historically, straw goods have been produced in Choiseul's smaller towns and have been a major source of revenue for artisans.

Locals' handcrafted straw goods are on display and available for purchase at the Choiseul Arts & Craft Center in La Farge.

This artisan center is a great location to get unique straw items, therefore we highly suggest stopping by. The crafts center personnel may also provide you the straw craftsmen' contact details.

To go about the island and see how these incredible handmade things are manufactured, ask a taxi driver for advice.

You may always go to the Vendor's Arcade in Castries if you are unable to attend the Choiseul

Arts and Craft Center. Products made by local artists may be found all throughout the island.

5. Pottery

St. Lucia produces skilled potters. People who live in parts of the island where clay is the most common soil choose to make clay products as a means of making money.

Cooking pans, coal pots for cooking, and flower pots were among the domestic items made originally of clay. Many potters eventually started selling their creations and turned it into a successful business.

Since potters have been transferring their knowledge and expertise to the next generation, it's likely that you may encounter clay objects while exploring the island or at your lodging.

Currently, it is almost difficult to see the process of creating clay items since it takes several days to dig up the clay, shape it, fire it in wood furnaces, and give it a stone-rubbed texture.

You may still purchase pre-made clay items to take home, however. Similar to wood carvings, we advise purchasing smaller clay items since they may be rather large and weighty.

In St. Lucia, Vin's Agri Tours is a tour operator that offers clay pottery manufacturing activities. If you want to make some clay crafts to bring back home, you may check out their website and get in touch with them!

Little bowls or flowerpots are excellent choices that will look wonderful and function well in your house for many years. The potters of St.

Lucian are well regarded worldwide, and you might be excited to get a product of such exquisite craftsmanship.

Like everything else we've covered, keep a look out for them when you browse the Vendor's Arcade or Castries Market.

Because clay goods may be extremely delicate, be care to wrap them appropriately before returning home.

When you go to St. Lucia, we hope that this list will be a valuable resource for you! International art and craft things are always wonderful keepsakes to bring home.

Markets and Shopping Districts

The greatest locations to shop in St. Lucia vary from multi-story malls with big brands to tiny, independent craft shops. The majority of small retailers would gladly assist you in finding personalized presents. You may also witness regional artisans and crafters at work at select locations.

You may find a variety of businesses together with breathtaking views of St Lucia's famous bays and verdant plantations. The best part, then? Numerous locations are duty-free. Remember to bring in your passport to get exclusive savings on luxury products.

1. Castries Central Market

Numerous restaurants, shops specializing in arts and crafts, and hundreds of booths offering locally grown vegetables can be found in the Castries Central Market. Given that it is more than a century old, it is understandable why this ancient marketplace is essential to St Lucian culture.

There will always be a boisterous welcome for you. It's an excellent place to snap selfies because of the famous clock tower façade. While the fresh produce area is a terrific location to buy for tropical fruits and veggies, the arts and crafts market is a treasure mine of presents and mementos. Visit the market on a Saturday morning when the people are out doing their weekly shopping if you want to feel the true energy of the place.

2. Baywalk Mall

Baywalk Mall is a contemporary retail center with more than fifty companies. This place offers an amazing selection of both domestic and foreign brands for clothing, accessories, trinkets, gadgets, and cosmetics. If you're searching for wine, cheese, and international foods, there's also an artisan supermarket.

When it's time for dinner, you may have pizza at Amici, sushi at Sakuragi, or Chinese food at Jade Terrace. For delicious handmade Italian ice cream, visit the beloved Elena's in the area. It's a terrific way to cool down after spending some time in the sun. Baywalk Mall is located near Rodney Bay, a well-liked vacation spot in St. Lucia.

3. JQ Rodney Bay Mall

One of the first retail complexes in St. Lucia, JQ Rodney Bay Mall has three floors and several stores. The first level is lined with a variety of cafés and eateries, while the upper floors include just about everything you could possibly need.

For tiny items you may forget while on vacation, the mall is a terrific place to shop. You may visit the on-site hairdresser to receive a haircut or go shopping for cozy clothing. If you're craving something familiar from home, there's an international supermarket. Also, a wide variety of presents and mementos for family members back home are available. Remember to carry your passport since JQ Rodney Bay Mall is duty-free, which is its finest feature.

4. Sea Island Cotton Shop

At Baywalk Mall, there is a duty-free fashion store called Sea Island Cotton Shop. Along with some name-brand apparel, it specializes on a variety of locally created beachwear, accessories, and gifts. If you're looking for some lightweight but durable shoes, the shop carries a nice assortment of REEF sandals.

Because to Sea Island Cotton Shop's reputation for duty-free sales, purchasing presents here is much less expensive than doing so at the airport. From vintage beer mugs to fridge magnets to locally crafted decorations, you can find something for everyone at home. If you wish to make certain Caribbean meals at home, there is even spicy pepper sauce available.

5. Diamonds International St. Lucia

A specialty retailer of watches and jewelry for the Caribbean is Diamonds International St. Lucia. It is located in the duty-free retail center Pointe Seraphine, which is close to Castries. Since 1988, it has been a well-known institution in St. Lucia, so you can count on excellent quality and service.

In addition to their own brand, DI Diamonds, Diamonds International St Lucia offers high-end jewelry from Crown of Light and Safi Kilima Tanzanite. You may select your chosen styles with the assistance of the experienced and helpful personnel. The free goodies that come with certain purchases are the nicest part.

6. Island Mix

Situated at Rodney Bay, a little distance south of Reduit Beach in St Lucia, Island Mix is an art gallery. It's understandable why artists come here to paint and sell their wares—the picturesque vistas of boats moored in the harbor are very appealing.

After perusing the regional artwork, you may relax with a drink at Island Mix's on-site café. This place is known for its regular fish fry nights, so check the internet schedule before you go. Freshly filtered coffee and a delicious daily menu are available in the café; we suggest trying it with a local rum cake.

7. St Lucia Rum Shop

Caribbean-wide award-winning rums are available at St Lucia Rum Shop. The little shop is located at Pointe Seraphine, which is just south of the George F. L. Charles Airport. The most popular drink in the Caribbean is rum, and this store offers more than you could ever sample in one visit.

Genuine rum enthusiasts need not to pass up the chance to get certain St Lucian specialties, including Admiral Rodney and Bounty. There are a ton of options available, including golden, dark, light, spicy, and anything in between. Professional staff members are eager to suggest a rum that matches your preferences, and the ambiance is always welcoming.

8. Choiseul Art Gallery

The skilled local artists of St Lucia showcase their distinctive paintings and handicrafts at the Choiseul Art Gallery. Situated about 1 km north of the Riviere Doree Sugar Mill Ruins, it is situated south of Choiseul.

The gallery has locally manufactured pottery, handcrafted decorations, and oil paintings depicting well-known St. Lucian landscapes. This place is as St. Lucian as it gets. If all you want to do is enjoy the art, the owner will be happy to explain how each item was made, and you are under no need to purchase.

9. Caribelle Batik

In St. Lucia, Caribelle Batik is a store that offers locally manufactured cotton textiles. Located in Castries, the boutique is tucked away among the Howelton Estate's tropical gardens. There are many activities in the region to do either before or after you buy.

Made in its basement workshop, Caribelle Batik employs the best cotton textiles available in the area. As you browse for your ideal Caribbean-inspired ensemble, you can see the artisans at their work. Additionally, the estate has other workshops that create regional specialties, like chocolate.

10. The Batik Studio

The Batik Studio is a shop and studio that offers a variety of clothing and artwork in the batik style. Every item is made on location, and the proprietor will be happy to walk you through the special batik painting technique.

In addition, batik wall hangings and covers are available for purchase at The Batik Studio. The batik designs give you a tropical atmosphere, while the Caribbean cotton keeps you cool in the sun. The shop is situated at Bouton, on St. Lucia's western coast.

Chapter 9: Practical Information

Health and Safety

Safety should always come first in everything that you do, particularly while visiting a foreign nation.

Making travel arrangements involves a lot, and it may easily go from an exciting to a stressful process. In a series of travel safety advices, I hope this offers useful information for your protection when visiting St. Lucia.

I'll break down all I can about currencies, weather, legislation, and transportation, among other things. While you arrange your vacation to St. Lucia, I want you to feel completely secure and confident.

You've come to the perfect site if you're already in St. Lucia and need advice on how to enjoy a worry-free or exciting yet safe holiday.

NOTE
While wall plugs in different accommodations in St. Lucia vary, British (220v) outlets are the most often used standard.

You may need an adaptor if you're traveling from the US in order to charge your electronics.

Likewise, as some hotel locations utilize US (120v) plugs, you can also have trouble finding charging sites if you are traveling from the UK.

Road Safety and Transportation

If renting a car is an option for you when you get to St. Lucia, it may be very cost-effective and convenient.

There are a few things to keep in mind, however. Since there isn't much traffic assistance in St. Lucia, drive carefully in crowded locations, especially those that are close to airports, schools, and enterprises, or popular retail destinations like Rodney Bay and Castries.

Pay attention to people crossing the street from windows or strolling along sidewalks, particularly in the above stated regions. Never, ever take up hitchhikers or strangers.

There are many turns and slopes to navigate on these very tiny roads. Don't worry if you don't feel comfortable driving these island roads;

hotels, malls, resorts, and excursions all provide taxi services.

Minibuses are another affordable and accessible form of public transportation. Remember that licensed taxi service cars have blue license plates, while public transit has green license plates, to help you distinguish between the two.

Valuables

I suggest leaving your valuables behind, such as your passport and pricey jewelry, when you check out of your hotel or other lodging.

It is imperative that you always keep these things securely packed in your baggage, regardless of whether you are visiting a five-star hotel or a little guesthouse.

If you're going on a brief vacation, it would be a fantastic idea to have a pouch that can be hidden by your shirt or blouse to carry your money, keys, and other essentials so you don't lose them.

A backpack or rucksack works well for going about for tours and other activities, but make sure you just bring what you really need so you're not completely lost if your preferred bag is lost.

Never venture out from busy places or go through empty streets in search of your destination.

Roaming and Exploring
St. Lucia offers many exploration opportunities, but you should always prioritize your safety.

With so many undiscovered gems, you want to book the greatest excursions, go in groups, and feel secure in the knowledge that you will return safely to your lodging.

It is advisable to get familiar with the roads and surroundings if you are renting a car. You may do this by getting printed maps from the hotel, using Google Maps, or even hiring a companion to accompany you on your journey.

I highly advise against venturing into uncharted territory without enough information of the region, since this puts you at risk of being lost or having your personal belongings taken.

If you want to spend the evening at a bar or street party, it's a good idea to think about having a designated driver, such a taxi driver.

It's a good idea to have the phone number stored for any villas, guest houses, or similar accommodations you may be staying at.

Illegal Substances and Attire

Cannabis is one of the substances that should be avoided when it comes to illicit substances, apart from the obvious ones like cocaine, since using or possessing marijuana might result in penalties in St. Lucia. If you traffic in these prohibited drugs, you will face consequences.

I drive on the left side of the road in St. Lucia, and you should always have your international driver's license with you while operating a vehicle.

Use your seat belt; if an officer of the law finds you not to, you will be punished.

When someone outside of the St. Lucian police force dons camouflage attire, it becomes illegal. It is also offensive to use textiles that are identical.

Medical Support

Public hospitals are Victoria Hospital in Castries and St. Judes Hospital in Vieux Fort.

As you may expect, there will be heavy traffic at these two hospitals, and you could have to wait a while to get help.

Tapion Hospital, a private healthcare facility close to Castries, offers timely care at a fee that may be high.

Make sure you pack with travel insurance that includes hospital stays before you go. You may be sent to Martinique or Miami to get the appropriate treatment if your injury is severe enough to need medical attention outside of St. Lucia.

Make sure your travel insurance covers medical evacuation in case of need.

Climate and Natural Disasters

The hurricane season runs from the middle of May to the end of November, so take that in mind when choosing your travel dates.

Although St. Lucia has been very fortunate not to have had any significant storms recently, you should be aware that your safety is our first priority.

Because tropical storms have a history of intensifying quickly into hurricanes, local services will alert you to weather updates well in advance, allowing you to take precautions before endangering your safety or ability to access services.

It is a good idea to be ready for everything and to have emergency contact information on hand for your airline, service providers, and any other services you may need or use while traveling.

In the unlikely event that a storm strikes while you are traveling, heed the guidance from our local emergency services and your lodging providers.

Currency and Banking

The Eastern Caribbean Dollar (EC$) is the currency used in Saint Lucia; however, it may be exchanged for and used on the island in replacement of US dollars.

Our banks provide a broad variety of currency conversion services, including the Canadian dollar, euro, and British pound.

Banks in Saint Lucia provide a comprehensive variety of banking and foreign exchange services. Most banks provide ATMs where you may use your credit or debit card to get cash in the Eastern Caribbean Dollar, the local currency. Typically, banks are open from 8:00 am to 2:00 pm, with some remaining open until 5:00 pm on Fridays. On Saturdays, banks are open from 8:00 a.m. until 12:00 p.m. at the Rodney Bay Marina.

Communication

In general, communication in St. Lucia is easy, and there are plenty of ways to keep in touch with loved ones, as well as for any business or vacation requirements. An outline of St. Lucia's communication alternatives is provided below:

1. Mobile Phone Services:
There is a robust mobile phone network in St. Lucia, and getting a local SIM card when you get there is not too difficult. Well-known service providers include Flow and Digicel. Make sure your phone can accept overseas SIM cards by unlocking it.

2. International Roaming:
Find out about overseas roaming possibilities from your service provider if you would rather use your home cell number. Recognize that roaming might be costly, so find out the prices ahead of time.

3. Wi-Fi:

Customers may choose to use free or paid Wi-Fi in a lot of motels, eateries, and coffee shops. Wi-Fi hotspots are also available at well-known tourist locations.

4. Internet Cafes:

While they are becoming less widespread, internet cafés are still possible to locate in cities and popular tourist destinations.

5. Postal Services:

Mail and parcels may be sent from St. Lucia via the postal service. There are minor post offices in different communities in addition to the main post office in Castries.

6. Emergency Services:

In St. Lucia, 999 is the emergency number for law enforcement, ambulance, and fire services.

7. Language:

The majority of people in St. Lucia speak English, which is the official language of the island. Apart from English, Kweyol, a Creole language rooted in French, is a commonly spoken language among Saint Lucians.

8. Local Calls:

Using a local SIM card or hotel landline, making local calls in St. Lucia is simple. Understand the area-specific calling codes.

9. International Calls:

You may use a local SIM card or your mobile phone with an international plan to make international calls from St. Lucia. Furthermore, a lot of hotels and phone booths have international calling capabilities.

10. Messaging Apps:

Well-known messaging services like Facebook Messenger and WhatsApp are useful for keeping in contact with loved ones back home and function well in St. Lucia.

Although communication services are commonly accessible, bear in mind that in some isolated or hilly locations, the quality of internet connection and cell coverage may differ. Before your journey to St. Lucia, it is essential to inquire about international prices and alternatives with your cell service provider.

Chapter 10: Tips for a Sustainable Visit

Responsible Tourism

The Caribbean island of Saint Lucia is regarded as a popular travel destination. To protect the island's nature and preserve its unspoiled beauty, it is crucial for visitors to behave responsibly. Here are some facts and viewpoints on responsible tourism in Saint Lucia that you should be aware of before traveling there.

Tourism in Saint Lucia
In general, one may argue that Saint Lucia has avoided the detrimental effects of widespread mass tourism because of its reputation for

trekking, birdwatching, and natural features. While there are resorts, growth has been inclusive and managed due to construction height restrictions and the "Queen's Chain," a statute that ensures Saint Lucian locals own and have access to beach properties. But if you're looking for peace and quiet, you'll have to go to other areas of the island since many resorts are located on the northern coastlines. Today, the majority of the island's revenue comes from tourism; yet, visitors to Saint Lucia need to exercise caution and behave appropriately while there.

The people and culture

Visitors will have the chance to participate in Saint Lucia Heritage Tourism, a program designed to raise awareness of the region's cultural heritage and put money into the hands of residents. As a result, many facets of Saint

Lucia's history are enhanced, including its colorful festivals, Amerindian archeology, and Creole food and cocoa plantations.

It's Saint Lucia's Creole Heritage month in October, so if you go there, you'll discover that local communities are holding a number of tourist-attracting activities all throughout the island. The town of Dennery, where freshly caught fish is prepared using traditional methods, is another fascinating destination. Along with the farmers, you may take a tour of nearby farms to learn about coffee, cocoa, and coconuts.

The environment and wildlife
The preservation of the Saint Lucia parrot, which is now both the national bird and a popular tourist destination, is an example of a local success story. The hawksbill, leatherback,

and green sea turtles, which lay their eggs on the island's coastlines, are among the other creatures that are in danger. Numerous reserves protect the mountains and jungles in the island's interior. You could think about taking interCaribbean Airways, which has links to several airports around the Caribbean islands, to Saint Lucia in order to take in the island's natural features.

Tips for responsible tourism

Enjoying experiences that help the community is an excellent way to practice responsible tourism. Some examples of these experiences include dining at local restaurants, hiking with a local guide, staying at guesthouses, and buying handcrafted goods made in the area. Being responsible means avoiding littering, reducing waste, and returning things like old batteries when you can. It is important to avoid touching fish, turtles, or coral while diving or snorkeling. You should also avoid trampling on fragile coral. Furthermore, if you want to go on a whale or dolphin watching cruise, confirm that the operator is reputable and adheres to safety procedures.

Eco-Friendly Practices

Eco-friendly and sustainable techniques are highly valued in St. Lucia in order to maintain the island's breathtaking natural beauty and save the environment. The following are a few eco-friendly activities and methods that you might see in St. Lucia:

Marine Conservation: Numerous marine conservation initiatives are in place in St. Lucia with the goal of safeguarding marine habitats and coral reefs. Responsible diving and snorkeling techniques are encouraged by several dive companies and organizations.

National Parks and Reserves: To preserve its natural assets, St. Lucia has created national parks and reserves. This comprises Pigeon Island National Landmark and the well-known Pitons Management Area. There are stringent conservation laws governing these places.

Sustainable Tourism: Sustainable tourism practices are a priority for a large number of St. Lucian hotels, resorts, and tour companies. They take steps to lessen their influence on the environment, such using water wisely, cutting waste, and using energy-efficient equipment.

Eco-Lodges: Eco-friendly lodging is available in St. Lucia, with hotels and resorts emphasizing sustainability. These properties often promote neighborhood communities, appropriately manage garbage, and use renewable energy sources.

Reforestation Projects: In an effort to stop deforestation and preserve its beautiful landscapes, St. Lucia has started reforestation efforts. The island's rainforests are protected, and sustainable forestry methods are promoted.

Green Certification: An international benchmark for environmentally friendly travel and tourism is the Green Globe Certification program. St. Lucian enterprises that are dedicated to environmentally friendly practices have been certified by Green Globe.

Recycling and Waste Management: There is an attempt to encourage recycling and conscientious disposal of garbage. Recycling programs are offered in certain places, and recycling bins are often located at popular tourist locations.

Solar Energy: Many areas of the island use solar energy for both business and domestic uses. Rooftop solar panels are a regular sight.

Local Sourcing: Local sourcing of products by restaurants and hotels helps to support local farmers and lessens the carbon footprint involved with importing commodities.

Conservation Education: In St. Lucia, there are several organizations and tour companies that provide educational tours and programs with an emphasis on sustainable practices and environmental protection. These encounters contribute to increasing knowledge of the island's distinctive ecosystems.

Protected Species: Sea turtles are among the many protected animals that call St. Lucia home. To save these creatures and their breeding grounds, conservation initiatives have been put in place.

You may support these eco-friendly initiatives while visiting St. Lucia by booking eco-friendly lodging, using eco-friendly tour companies, and acting as a conscientious tourist by reducing your environmental footprint. To ensure that St. Lucia's natural beauty is preserved for future generations, abide by local laws and conservation initiatives.

Chapter 11: Language and Culture

Creole Phrases

St. Lucian Creole, also known as Kweyol or Patois, is a French-based Creole language spoken on the island of St. Lucia. Here are some common Creole phrases and expressions that you might find useful or interesting:

Wè sa? - (Way sa?) - "What's that?"

Bonjou - (Bon-zhoo) - "Good morning."

Bonswa - (Bon-swa) - "Good evening" or "Good night."

Kòmantwé yé? - (Ko-man-tweh yay?) - "How are you?"

Mwen byen, mèsi - (Mwen byen, meh-see) - "I'm fine, thank you."

Sa ka fèt? - (Sa ka fay?) - "What's happening?" or "What's going on?"

Menm si - (Menm see) - "Even if" or "Although."

Kòmant t'apé kouri? - (Ko-man ta-peh koo-ree?) - "How was the run?"

Kouman ou ka di sa an Kweyol? - (Koo-man oo ka dee sa an Kweyol?) - "How do you say that in Kweyol?"

Mwen pa konprann - (Mwen pa kon-pran) - "I don't understand."

Demen - (Deh-men) - "Tomorrow."

Lajan - (Lah-zhan) - "Money."

Mwen renmen ou - (Mwen ren-men oo) - "I love you."

Tout moun - (Too moon) - "Everyone" or "Everybody."

Kote ou rete? - (Ko-teh oo ret) - "Where do you live?"

Ou byen konnen isit la - (Oo byen koh-nen ee-see lah) - "You know it here well."

Nonm - (Non) - "Man" or "Male."

Fanm - (Fahm) - "Woman" or "Female."

Poukisa? - (Poo-kee-sa) - "Why?"

Konbyen sa koute? - (Ko-byen sa koot?) - "How much does it cost?"

Keep in mind that St. Lucian Creole has regional variations, and pronunciation may be slightly different between communities. Learning a few Creole phrases can be a fun way to connect with locals and immerse yourself in the island's culture during your visit to St. Lucia.

St. Lucia Creole Proverbs

Grandparents give our lives a unique flavor. The majority of us have happy recollections of spending Easter or the summer vacations someplace in the countryside with them.

Our elders undoubtedly had a wealth of knowledge to share. They would constantly impart a "saying" in order to convey a crucial societal lesson, advice, or warning. Without a doubt, these "sayings" have ingrained themselves into our culture, and the majority of Saint Lucians are proficient at using them generally.

These creole proverbs are among the wisest ones our ancestors have told us.

1. **'Shee vay tac tac':** when you've brushed your hair and there is one hair which defies taming and stands straight up with a zig zag nature all its own.

2. **'peeyops':** a derogatory term meaning you are "losing your marbles"

3. **'meme bête meme pwel':** literally translates to "same beast same hair" meaning the same creature, meaning "we are the same", or "what you have just said is the same as what I've just said"

4. **'shease':** cheap. Unwilling to spend any money.

5. 'mackawel': literally translates to "Boa Constrictor" but means that feeling of fullness and need to rest after eating too much. This is because a Boa when it has feasted needs to rest for days to digest the whole animal it has consumed.

6. 'Co shee': crooked

7. 'zeeay coh key': cross eyed

8. 'bazoudi': stunned dazed

9. 'Kabwit by ball ek se mouton ki sou': goat at a party and its sheep thats drunk

10. 'Avan Zaboca te ca bon, makak te ca know petit ee': before avocado is ripe, monkey is taking for its young. Before I had I was managing. Now I'm taking before I need.

11. 'Sacwe tonnaire': sacred thunder an expletive similar in tone to "hells bells", wooy, for heaven's sake

12. 'Chat pas ca fait chien': cat doesn't do dog, meaning a person will behave according to their "type"

13. 'Koul koutla pas ni mak en glo': cutlass lash doesn't mark water or what the eye doh see doh grieve the heart.

14. 'Pwan douvan, avan douvan pwan ou': take in front before in front takes you. In other words make preparations for the "storm" before the "storm" catches you out.

15. Sé asou chimiz blan nou kawè tach: Those who appear as most righteous are often the ones more susceptible to scandals.

16. Twou manti pas fon: You don't have to look far for the truth to be revealed.

17. Anyen pa gwatis an lavi sala. Pa kwennen ko'w. Tout bagay ni an pwi ében an sakwifis: Nothing is for free in this life. Don't fool yourself. Everything has a price or a sacrifice.

18. Si ou ni an bagay pou di, annèk di'y las jété pawol: If you have something to say, just say it. Stop throwing shade.

19. Bèl flè san lòdè: Pretty face with bad character.

20. Fè sa ki dwèt pa sa ki ézé: Do what is right, not what is easy.

21. An kay ki ka koulé sa kwennen solèy-la mé I pas sa kwennen lapli-a: A person's mistakes will be exposed sooner or later.

22. Chien pa fè chat: The child isn't different from their parent (the apple does not fall far from the tree).

23. Chat pas là wat ka bi bal: There is no one around, so you're taking advantage.

24. Sa ou fè se sa ou wè: The things that you do now will come back to you.

Cultural Etiquette

ACCESSING CARIBBEAN CULTURAL ETIQUETTE

Indulging in the rich and varied cultures of the Caribbean will improve your vacation experience as you set off on your voyage. You need to be aware of the customs and traditions of any place you visit in order to have a civil and pleasant conversation with the inhabitants.

This chapter will cover a number of topics, including the significance of honoring regional traditions and customs, advice on how to greet people and use basic language, tips and gratuities, dress regulations, and acceptable clothing. You'll develop deep relationships with Caribbean people and help to preserve their history and customs by adopting cultural etiquette.

Respecting Local Customs and Traditions

Research and Learn

Completing your studies is the first step towards being a considerate traveler. Spend some time learning about the traditions and cultural norms of the particular Caribbean location you'll be visiting before you board the aircraft. Every island has its own set of customs that are shaped by its topography, history, and the many civilizations that have converged there.

Examine a range of sources, such as internet discussion boards and travel guides, to get insight into the customs, values, and possible taboos of the area. This might include picking up tips on proper eating manners, knowing what to wear in certain settings, or comprehending the importance of particular customs or holidays. You can travel with ease and civility and prevent inadvertent offense if you have a rudimentary awareness of these factors.

Observe and Follow

When you visit the Caribbean, observe how the people there behave. They are the finest sources of advice on proper manners, so you may navigate new circumstances by following their lead. This might be seeing how people behave with one another, how they dress in different contexts, or how they approach places of worship and cultural significance.

One essential component of manners is respect. Be mindful of religious places and customs. When visiting churches or temples, dress accordingly. Sacred spaces should be kept silent. Always get permission before taking pictures of people or private property. This respects people's right to privacy and their ability to manage their public persona.

Engage and Learn

Ultimately, the chance to interact with the locals is the most fulfilling aspect of any trip. Seize the chance to get firsthand knowledge about their customs and traditions. Take part in regional celebrations, as they provide a lively glimpse into the customs and collective identity of the area. See the distinctive crafts made in the area and sample some of the traditional cuisine sold at the local markets.

Seek for genuine cultural encounters that will help you comprehend and appreciate the way of life there. This may be striking up a discussion with the locals, taking up a traditional craft, or learning how to dance. Recall that experiencing a local culture involves more than simply watching; it also entails actively participating and picking up knowledge.

In the Caribbean, etiquette entails more than merely abiding by the rules. It's about immersing oneself in the experience, learning from the community, and showing respect for the local way of life. Investigating, taking in, and participating enhance your trip experience and help create a more civilized and compassionate world society.

Greetings and Basic Phrases in the Local Language

Greetings: The First Step to Connection

Acquiring fundamental greetings in the native tongue is the first and potentially crucial step towards proficient communication. Saying "hello," "good morning," or "good afternoon" in the native language might help you connect with locals and create a more meaningful conversation.

Knowing how to say "thank you" is helpful in addition to these polite pleasantries. Expressing gratitude in the local tongue helps personalize your encounters since it is a global language that cuts across cultural boundaries.

Before your travel, practice these words, and don't be scared to use them. Even a few words or sentences spoken in the local tongue may make a big difference to the locals. Recall that effective communication involves more than simply using words; it also entails being respectful of and interested in the cultures of others.

Politeness: A Universal Language

Beyond just saying hello, learning certain courteous terms and expressions in the native tongue can improve your communication considerably. Even though they appear straightforward, phrases like "please," "pardon me," and "I'm sorry" have a lot of meaning.

In every culture, these expressions are fundamental instruments of deference and thoughtfulness. Using them shows that you are aware of and respectful of local customs and etiquette, which may help you build positive connections with new individuals you meet.

Once again, don't stress about using proper language or pronunciation. Here, respect for the local way of life and a desire to interact with it are more important than fluency.

Tipping and Gratuities

Understand Local Practices

Tipping traditions may differ greatly across nations and even between areas of the same nation. It is crucial for conscientious travelers to learn about the customs around tipping in their destination. While some Caribbean islands depend on direct gratuities to service professionals, others may add a service fee in the bill.

To acquaint yourself with the customs, seek for trustworthy travel books or internet sites that provide tipping guidelines relevant to each nation. Recognize the appropriate tipping % or amount for various settings, including hotels, restaurants, and while using tour guides or taxi services.

Remember that these standards are sometimes arbitrary, and the precise amount may vary depending on the caliber of the assistance obtained. Nonetheless, being aware of the basics can help you avoid unpleasant situations when you tip too much or too little.

Show Appreciation

Tipping is more than just a means to express gratitude for excellent service. Your gratuities help the local economy, especially in areas where tips constitute a significant portion of the pay for service personnel.

If you are served very well, show your appreciation by leaving a large tip. This encourages the person to keep up their great job and rewards them for their efforts.

Recall that leaving a tip is a method to show respect and gratitude in addition to being a business transaction. Tipping may be a straightforward way to express thanks, even in situations when communication is difficult.

Dress Code and Appropriate Attire

Respect Cultural Sensitivities
Clothing serves as more than simply a physical covering in many regions of the globe; it also serves as a representation of social conventions, religious beliefs, and cultural values. Therefore, it's imperative to observe local dress regulations and wear modest clothing, particularly when visiting places of worship or conservative neighborhoods.

For example, visitors to numerous holy locations are required to cover their knees and shoulders. Wearing provocative or exposing apparel might be seen as disrespectful in certain cultures. It is thus wise to acquaint yourself before your visit with the customs of the area. This guarantees that you are at ease and dressed correctly for the environment while also demonstrating respect for the culture.

Always remember that it's preferable to err on the side of humility. Always have a scarf or shawl on available in case you need to cover yourself in an unforeseen circumstance.

Adapt to the Environment

The temperature and environment of your location should be taken into account while selecting your outfit. Cotton and linen are excellent alternatives since they are lightweight and breathable, especially in the Caribbean, which is renowned for its tropical temperature. Many tropical places have bright colors, which are a reflection of the vivid native flora and culture.

Make sure you have the right attire and footwear if you want to partake in any particular activities, such as trekking or visiting rainforests. For example, wearing long trousers and strong shoes on a trip can shield you from insects and unforgiving terrain, while a rain jacket may be useful in a jungle.

In summary

You may develop close relationships with the people and learn more about their rich history by adopting cultural etiquette in the Caribbean. Recognize and respect cultural norms and traditions, pick up some basic greetings in the language, and be aware of clothing requirements. Tipping and gratuities are a great way to express gratitude and support the community's businesses and service providers.

Allow cultural etiquette to serve as your compass while visiting the colorful Caribbean countries. It will lead you to genuine encounters, reciprocal respect, and an incredibly immersive experience. You will leave a lasting impression and have a good influence on the communities you come into contact with by encouraging respect and cultural understanding.

Conclusion

St. Lucia provides an amazing Caribbean experience with its striking natural beauty, lively culture, and kind people. As our tour of this amazing island comes to a conclusion, we hope you've been motivated to discover its verdant jungles, unwind on its immaculate beaches, and take in the distinctive fusion of French, African, and Caribbean customs.

St. Lucia's renowned Pitons, glistening seas, and environmentally conscious lifestyle demonstrate the island's dedication to protecting its natural treasures. It offers a true experience of Caribbean life with its vibrant street celebrations, cultural events, and delectable food.

St. Lucia offers enough to offer, regardless of your preference for adventure, leisure, or a combination of the two. Enjoying delectable Creole cuisine and zip-lining over the trees are just two of the many ways that this place celebrates life and the natural world. Take with you the warmth and joie de vivre of St. Lucia together with your recollections of its picturesque surroundings as you depart from this enchanted island. From the beautiful paradise of St. Lucia, till we cross paths again, good bye.

Printed in Great Britain
by Amazon